FROM THE
LIBRARY OF

EMIL B.
FRIES

A Shop
in the High Street

A Shop in

SYBIL LEEK

the High Street

DECORATIONS BY DOUGLAS HALL

DAVID McKAY COMPANY, INC. • NEW YORK

A SHOP IN THE HIGH STREET

FIRST AMERICAN EDITION 1964

LIBRARY OF CONGRESS CATALOG CARD NUMBER: 64-15886

MANUFACTURED IN THE UNITED STATES OF AMERICA

Dedicated

to my large family,

the most important influence in the life

of a business woman

Contents

CONTENTS

I

You too
can have a lease

IT DROPS through the letter-box with a more pretentious sound than a bill or an income-tax demand note. Even from inside the lengthy thick envelope it gives out a faint odour of sanctimonious red-tape—a symbol of an age when a man's word is as nothing unless clothed in the panoply of archaic legal language. This is the day you have been waiting for—the arrival of the lease —a document more binding than a modern marriage licence and twice as dangerous as a decree nisi! Now is the time to take stock of the situation, to appraise the past weeks which have led to the arrival of this portentous document, a last chance to recant or advance. All you wanted was a little shop in the High Street!

Remember how you first saw the shop—a mass of elderly bricks and mortar, with wavy moss-laden roof tiles, in the middle of the High Street of a market town. In its emptiness it had a forlorn little-boy-lost air amongst the bustle of the other occupied shops. There was an urgency in you to know more about it and so you found someone who knew the last tenant, who knew the agent, who knew the secretary of the present landlord. Then followed innumerable 'phone calls, a mention of references, 'when did you last see your father' and 'are you respectable', and—at last—you have an order to view and the key to the door.

Forget the lingering sad smell of emptiness, the inevitable khaki-brown-green paint, the peeling wallpapers, the ominous sound of wooden floors crumbling beneath your feet—a sure indication of woodworm. Look beyond all this and see the impact of your own personality conquering the gloom and emerging in pristine splendour—a phoenix arising. At this stage it is essential to be optimistic; falter to give prudent thought to the wood-worm and all is lost! Fall violently in love with the sad, peeling walls as the paper sighs gently in every passing draught; walk in clouds of trailing glory or for ever forget this shop in the High Street.

Now is the time for the landlord to emerge into your life. From the well-protected cocoon of Big Business he comes—hitherto a voice on a telephone, disembodied from reality! From the pampered institution of a well-regulated office, protected from the public by an attentive secretary, he emerges to view *you*, his potential tenant. Now you have an affinity to a fly in a spider's web and can only struggle weakly to make a good impression. In later years, as you become more blasé about renting a place, you will realize how important it is to choose your landlord, equally as important as choosing your property, and with care you will eliminate this first frightening 'fly in the web' feeling.

Once in a misguided moment I attempted to negotiate for a property owned by a Trust. I should have known better and can only file the facts away under the heading of 'Experience—Unpleasant'! Certainly I cannot recommend any serious collector of leases ever to attempt to do business with such a concern. It is as abortive as negotiating with Dracula for the lease of a church-yard. In my case I received a well-typed letter announcing grace-fully that 'our Mr. Mason' would visit Ringwood to discuss such and such property with me.

'Our Mr. Mason' duly presented himself, a well-groomed but ageing young man with a particularly distressing voice. I felt that he was so obviously 'trained' to deal with clients, and any ideas which he may have had of his own had been technically ground down until he mouthed only the opinions of his masters. A modern Uriah Heap, well fed and well cared for, but still the Uriah Heap of the modern nine-to-five Welfare State type.

Over lunch at the local hotel, doubtless lulled into a momentary false state of security following one British sherry, I did

manage to discover that 'our Mr. Mason' had an aunt in Tun-
bridge Wells. The knowledge afforded the poor man no satisfaction and it so obviously pained him to think about her that I
tried to salvage the conversation by throwing in an aunt of mine
who lived in Brazil, until I remembered that she married a man
who kept a high-class brothel. In the nick of time I realized that I
was a 'potential' tenant of the Trust and this would probably have
acted as a deterrent to any proposed lease. Long before we had
reached the coffee stage at lunch all attempts at conversation had
died a natural death.

He was a meticulous young man. Before we left the table he
solemnly dragged out the neatest of little diaries and made a care-
ful note of the cost of the meal—doubtless for his all-important
expense account. It was all terribly sad. I longed desperately for
something to redeem his poor soul, for ever lost in the vested
interests of the Trust. The best I can say for him is that I am sure
he was and still is a most honest and virtuous employee, who
never added an unscrupulous penny to his legitimate expense
account. But I could never have faced a fourteen-year lease with
his firm. Imagine being descended upon at varying future dates
by a series of similar young men, all replicas of 'our Mr. Mason',
all virtuously serving in their robot well-trained fashion the
mysterious Trust. Goodbye Mr. Mason—for ever goodbye.

This unhappy experience served to teach me to choose my
landlord carefully and *never* to deal with the Uriah Heaps of the
world. All business for me must be strictly at the Summit—let
minion meet minion, but not for me.

Again, I have always tried to steer clear of the bluff, hearty
type of landlord—generally the local butcher who has done rather
well for himself. Beware of this type. He will treat you like a
daughter and call you 'meluv' when first you meet. At the
faintest sign of trouble he will bawl you down in a hard Northern
accent whilst still calling you 'luv' and will certainly end his
conversation by saying 'I'm a blunt man' or 'I've no hard feelings'.

No, for my part, if there is an element of choice I would choose
the lean saturnine type every time—a gentleman from the first

glass of sherry. When the time comes for a battle of wills—and, believe me, it always comes—he is a worthy opponent. No bawling or loss of face need arise and the sordid subject of drains and sewers can be skirmished with the equanimity of two experienced players enjoying a game of chess.

Beware, however, of too much charm on the part of your landlord. Always remember that he has something to sell and is looking for a good tenant and that charm is part of his stock-in-trade. Remember that an empty shop is as serious as a blot on his family escutcheon; a loss of dividend and a constant worry to his secretary and accountant. So charm is an undoubted asset. Never lose touch with the fact that the pleasantries of that first (and probably last) lunch engagement when you met to discuss in a civilized manner can give way to a peculiar state when he becomes your enemy. Remember that in a state of extreme emergency it is he who can marshal the heavy forces of the law— the big battalions—to his side, and not you. So before you enter this world of leases I advise you to learn to play chess and then you will never underestimate your opponent or your landlord.

Well, you pass the test as a potential tenant and believe me it isn't the look in your bonny blue eyes but merely your financial status that is the deciding factor. If you are a good gilt-edged investment, and equal to 10 per cent of anyone's capital outlay, then the little shop in the High Street is as good as yours. In the world of Big Business, what appears to you as an ecstatic vision is merely a matter of L.S.D.

Now you have reached the stage when a third party is drawn into the affair. Enter the villain in the form of a solicitor. He is the cleverest of the trio, for he is the man who has learnt the technique of winning on both the swings and the roundabouts. After assuring you that he is 'honoured' to act on your behalf, he becomes responsible for the document you have just taken out of the letter-box—the beautiful, desperate, all-embracing, completely bewildering and utterly illogical *lease*.

From past experience I never read a lease until Sunday afternoon; even if it arrives by the first post Monday morning I resolutely hide it away until the quietness of Sunday afternoon descends.

After all, let us face it, what else can you do on any English Sunday afternoon except read your leases? The moments before appending your signature to the fateful document should be savoured and every dreg of enjoyment dragged from them. So the scene should be set very carefully. Preferably, I send the children to their grandmamma's for the day, as there is no need for their simple minds to be burdened too soon by the more sordid passages of any lease. After all, the little shop in the High Street is meant only to be a home for them. Let them remain in ignorance for a little while that a home and a business needs a legal licence. Too soon will disillusion enter their lives. I like to study my leases with suitable background music. I have personal preference for the flamenco guitar music of Sabicas. In me this evokes a pleasant state of mellow nostalgia for leases of the past, but there is sufficient 'beat' in the music to keep the mind alert. Sometimes a simple drink in the shape of a bottle of subtle Sauterne will help to gloss through the more dismal passages. Do not, I beg you, ever undertake the reading of a lease whilst under the influence of gin—it promotes suicidal tendencies.

Here alone with your lease on a typical wet English Sunday afternoon you have within your own household the ingredients for a play, with the solicitor as the producer. Enter in the first act, the Lessor, magnificent in heavy red and black type—in other words, the Landlord, who is alternately the hero and the villain. Here, dear lady, in slightly less important type, is the Lessee, and that means *you*. A pitiful minion in the world of Big Business, a cog in the wheel yet as essential as a heroine in a romance.

Should you be a well-educated type of woman you will never, *but never* sign a lease. For you will have been taught, and quite rightly too, that you must never sign your name to anything that you do not understand, and you will *never* understand a lease. So you have to choose between being a party to a great legalized lie or not having a shop in the High Street. It is as simple as that; the choice is entirely yours, just as in Russian roulette.

When you reach a mention of the Arbitration Act of 1950 you are on the brink of the exquisite moment of truth. Pause delicately here, take a pen in your hand and in the presence of a reliable witness sign your name. Sign that the plate-glass window, even if non-existent, will be maintained by you; sign that in fourteen years' time you solemnly undertake to leave the place in the same state of repair as it is when you sign the lease (think of the peeling wallpapers and wonder how you will ever get it back to this state even in fourteen years of concentrated attack); sign, dear lady, and behold—you are now the proud possessor of a lease.

If you hear hollow laughter ringing through the rooms when you enter your shop in the High Street do not be afraid, for it is only a few fugitive fairies from the bottom of your landlord's garden. They are just stirring the woodworm into action to make sure that you never have a dull moment in all the next fourteen years of your life. You are on the verge of a great experience from which you will emerge a much wiser person. And all you wanted was a shop in the High Street!

2
From demon builders
and poltergeists—HELP!

I AM not the type of woman who can ever be called 'handy about the house'. Even spring cleaning is an anathema, to allow me to use a pot of paint and a brush is quite fatal, although the family are the first to admit that I am keen and industrious. I can make quite a small pot of paint go a very long way but the result is never quite what I intend. I dream of a day when I can send my family away for a picnic and on their return, my face glowing with pride, I can swing open the kitchen door and say, 'Look what I've been doing whilst you've all been out enjoying yourselves—doesn't the kitchen look wonderful?'

I imagine them looking into the kitchen, dazed by the gleaming new paint, ready to praise the work of dear old Mum, but it never works out like this. The last time I tried my hand at the sort of thing that any woman can do with the 'paint that any woman can use' and the brush that any woman finds easy to handle (so say the adverts, and surely they can't be wrong?) I achieved a new low rating for creating disaster. My eldest boy entered the kitchen, gave a sharp squeal, shut the door quickly and said with a certain sad wisdom, 'I'd better give you a hand with this mess before Dad sees it.' He is a sensible sporting child and tidied up beautifully, doing swift magical things with an old razor-blade round the inside of the window-frames, and he touched up the tear-streaked doors with an absolute touch of genius about him.

'Don't ever do anything like that again, Mum.' He sounded far too grim for his tender years.

When the lease of the shop in the High Street was duly signed I was faced with the problem of a great deal of necessary reconstruction. It is a vast spread-eagling house with very large rooms, every one of which has high ceilings. Most of the rooms have communicating doors in them and I was delighted with the amount of space—there seemed to be acres of floor and even miles of wall space. To counteract these advantages there was no lavatory indoors at all, no bathroom or kitchen. A quaint outdoor closet made me ponder as to what would happen if one slept on the third floor of the house and perhaps had just the tiniest suspicion of cystitus!

I decided that some very able-bodied man would have to undertake the construction of a modern kitchen, a bathroom and at least one lavatory must be inside the house. After all, we are in the High Street of a thriving market town. I 'phoned a builder whom I had known some time ago. At my urgent plea he duly reported to the house. He eyed each room with a jaundiced air. 'Ha,' he sniffed. 'There's a rare lot of work to be done here, *Mother*.' To this day I shall never know why this builder, who is old enough to be my father, insists on calling me 'Mother'. He is of North Country origin and maybe it is just an old friendly custom, or perhaps I am something which the psychiatrists call a 'mother image', representing something that my little builder had missed in his now long-forgotten youth. Anyway, from the first day I met him to the day when I finally paid the last of his bills he always referred to me as 'Mother'. At Christmas I am always tempted to send him a card loaded with robins and tinsel and sign it 'Your loving Mother'. I told him that it was essential to have an indoor lavatory, a hot-water system and some assemblance of hygienic amenities, and that I would like it done at once if not sooner.

'There's a lot of work here, Mother,' said the builder. 'I'll have to think a bit about it.'

It seemed practical to adapt this large building into two flats on the upper floors, leaving the downstairs quarters to be used as an annexe to the shop and to provide additional storage space. I remembered to ask for an estimate for the total amount of work which we had decided must be done, and in due course a lengthy document arrived in which the words 'making good' appeared with some monotony. I could not understand all the details, but on 'phoning the builder he assured me that all he had done was to write down in builders' language all that I had requested to be done in my crude basic English. I took his word for it. It was the figures at the end of the jargon that really frightened me. I studied them from every angle and finally came to the conclusion that this was the actual amount of hard cash which would be needed. It was a nerve-racking experience. After all, it was only reconstruction that I needed to be done, not a completely new building. Since that first estimate I have got used to shocks like this—that estimate was a mere bagatelle, a sort of softening-up account for much worse ones were to follow.

I told the builder to proceed, after a little broken pleading on my part about those ghastly figures at the end of the estimate. He was a very hard-headed North Countryman, this builder.

'There's a lot of work here, Mother.' He emphasized his point by poking bits of plaster away from the door-jambs. 'Of course, if you fancy trying anyone else . . .' I hastened to assure him that I would truly love him to do the work for me, that I was sure that no one else would do such a good job at such a splendidly *cheap* price. We drank a flask of tea together and sealed the deal.

Within the space of twelve telephone calls, varying from pleas to threats on my part, the builder finally moved in. He spent a whole day actually moving in; he set up large iron instruments, which looked like fugitives from an inquisition, in the room that was ultimately to be the lounge. Then he went to work. He ripped and tugged, pulled and tore. He swore robustly when floorboards refused to yield or became covered in showers of plaster descending on him in an unwary moment. But, my goodness, he worked. In three weeks we had a bathroom and lavatory and a magnificent modern kitchen on the first floor. On the top storey we had a kitchenette and a copper cylinder with an electric immersion heater in it. I never saw him wave a fairy wand over the place but he achieved the same result. We became great friends over thousands of cups of tea. I became on positively intimate terms with the newest types of pipes for bathrooms and the advantages of 'low suites' was discussed with great solemnity. I also learnt of the many terrible things that happened in Other People's Houses, necessitating the immediate calling in of our little builder. He was obviously conditioning me for the many things which would inevitably happen to me in this barn of a house.

'You'll be needing to get a decorator next week, Mother,' said the amiable builder; 'I'll have finished here, bar getting out my gear.'

The monstrous task of transforming the greenish-khaki paintwork into something more harmonious loomed formidably in front of me. In the town I knew that it was a matter of conjecture as to when the interior of this house had last been decorated. Some very old folks said they could remember it being done when they were at school themselves, others swore that there wasn't a man or woman alive who could reliably swear that it had been done during their lifetime.

It looked about like that too. The problem to outdate all other problems was upon me.

I decided that a naive approach to the builder might be useful.

'Oh,' I said, 'I hoped you were going to do the whole thing for me.'

The builder descended from the top step of his ladder with exaggerated delicate care, holding a length of copper piping in his hand. He tilted his cap backwards on his head and used the copper piping to indicate the shabby walls of the house.

'What, me?' he said. 'Me, do this?' (the copper pipe snaked from pointing at the wall to the ceiling). 'I'm a builder, *not* a decorator.'

He made it sound as if I'd accused him of some frightfully improper thing. Obviously there is a distinction between a builder and a decorator.

'Well, surely you know someone who could do the job for

me.' I tried to purr the words sweetly, believing that this was one of the times when a Lonely Little Helpless Woman act was really necessary. Even a bathroom, lavatory and modern kitchen would not compensate me for the khaki paint and peeling walls if the builder deserted me now.

'Perhaps you have a friend who would be glad of a job?' I pressed the matter. 'Surely you know someone? . . .'

I could hear little wheels going round in his head as he calculated the discount he would get by putting in a decorator that he knew.

'Aye, maybe I can.'

There seemed no point in further conversation. I could see that he was itching to do something with the copper piping, so I left him, praying hard that he would indeed produce someone quickly to do something to the horror of the walls. Everything seemed so much worse than when the lease had been signed.

Next day the builder appeared with a most peculiar little man with a startling fuzz of curly ginger hair.

'I've got him, Mother,' said the builder, pushing the poor little man forward as if he wished to show off some unique specimen that he had captured. Ginger-head shuffled forward.

'So you're going to decorate this barn of a place for me?' I queried.

The ginger-head rocked frantically. I began to feel sorry for him. Such a tiny man to tackle this huge fiend of a place.

I told him that I wanted everything done in grey and white. He showed no emotion at the suggestion but I took the odd shake of the ginger-head to mean that he agreed.

'How much can you do it for?' I asked.

'It's a big job . . .' The words drifted languidly from him and I could see that now he was gripped by some strong emotion. Perhaps he was a slow starter and had only just fully taken in the state of the walls. They would have appalled a much stronger-hearted creature than this fragile piece of manhood. All the pity I felt for him disappeared as he went on in a much stronger voice.

'*It's a very big job.*'

I was getting so used to words like this I now translated them as meaning that I could not expect anyone to do any job for me at anything except an exorbitant price. As the remains of a once healthy bank balance sheet unrolled itself before me, I said somewhat absent-mindedly,

'You'd better call me "Mother" as Mr. Henry does.'

The ginger-head recoiled as if it had been shot by the arrow of an erratic William Tell, shooting on one of his off-days.

'Beg pardon,' said the shocked voice of the aspiring decorator.

'Oh, it doesn't matter,' I said, as I realized that he was shaken. After all, he was such a nervous little thing that I wanted only to make him feel at home. Actually, I fancied him less as a foster-son than I did the builder, although he was possibly younger.

'Just start as soon as possible.'

He started. He attacked the place as if he hated it. He destroyed the green-khaki paint with the skilful quick strokes of a commercial Rembrandt. He ripped and tore at the walls as if he had to get some desperate destructive element out of his sytem. From this frightening outburst of quite vicious energy he achieved success. Two weeks later we were a gleaming shimmering mass of virgin white walls and grey paint.

It was a wonderful feeling to switch on the new electric heater and get hot water, to pull chains where none had ever been pulled before and finally to plan the rooms.

I set the kitchen out first with some fine old oak pieces. I had the urge to reproduce a quaint 'olde worlde' type of kitchen, with lots of copper pans and earthenware dishes. I placed rush-bottomed chairs with ladder backs around a two-hundred-year-old oak table. Copper jelly moulds graced the topmost ledge of a fine pine dresser. Another dresser flaunted a fair selection of blue-and-white pottery mostly of traditional willow pattern, which is the finest foil for old oak. Finally I threw up a bed in another room and moved in.

Eight days later I sold the entire kitchen as it stood to an American buyer and I've never again been able to achieve the same effect or such a satisfying result as with the oak and pine of those first early days. I consoled myself that the cheque paid for a great deal of the builder's work, but I felt quite ill when the removal men heaved the dressers away. I shrugged the feeling away by thinking that I would soon get another one. I did, within two days, but, alas, it never even reached the kitchen, for I sold it as it was being unloaded into the covered porch. Since then I have given up trying to make a real 'olde-worlde' kitchen. As I write this we have a jumble of furniture in the kitchen—clean, neat and very utilitarian, without that first slush of glamour.

It was a lovely kitchen whilst it lasted, though!

During the weeks when the builder and the decorator had been waging war on the upstairs I had been filling in the time between making cups of tea with fitting out the shop. It was only when I started to write this book that I remembered that I never had the shop decorated at all. In the excitement of getting the major part of the house done, and with full-blooded eagerness to set out the shop, I neglected to do a thing in it. I had been merrily stacking furniture against the walls 'to see what they looked like'. I hung things from the ceiling, and in tiny places high up on the walls where the furniture does not reach I had put pictures and decorated plates. Then suddenly I was too busy to think ever again about peeling wallpaper. Sometimes when I have sold a plate or picture from the wall I have had to hasten to put something else into position, but it was so easy to do. I doubt if I shall ever now be able to make the effort of having the shop decorated. It would be a major operation which I think would be beyond me.

I met the builder one day later. We stood on the opposite side of the road to the shop gazing at the building.

'Mother,' he said seriously, 'Mother, one day you're going to have trouble with that there roof of yours.'

I followed the direction of his eyes. I've always loved our wavy roof with its mature autumn brown-shaded tiles which blend so beautifully with the rest of the High Street.

'Mark my words, Mother,' he said, screwing up his eyes and scratching his ear. 'Them old tiles is going to come aslithering off one day, and then you'm in for it. . . . ' He slurred the last words as if he enjoyed the prospect of anyone's roof coming 'aslithering off'.

I regret to say that shortly afterwards the roof did slide off, causing a rare amount of panic in me and resulting in numerous 'phone calls to my landlord. The dear man came over himself to view the damage and announced that all he could do would be to put a new roof on the place. He was very much calmer about the whole thing than I was. After all, whilst he had been snug in his luxurious house in the better part of Bournemouth I had spent the whole of Boxing Day rescuing furniture and mopping up pools of water. There had been a storm on Christmas night; in the early hours of Boxing Day I was awakened by my youngest son shouting:

'Come quickly, Mummy, the roof's fallen in.'

I thought he was having a nightmare and at first took no notice. After all, following a hearty Christmas anyone is apt to have the hazy feeling that it doesn't really matter if the roof does fall in!

I didn't know as much about our roof on that morning as I do now, otherwise I wouldn't have lingered so long in bed before going out to attend to the debris. Our landlord kept his promise to send men along to deal with the problem of the slipping roof. One New Year's Day I arrived home after a trip to Somerset to find the shop in the High Street encased in a huge steel corset from which several red lamps leered with bloodshot eyes through the evening mist as I approached the shop.

'But no . . .' I reasoned, 'it just isn't possible, they don't have such things in England.' Truly those red lights worried me; one is bad enough, but six of them, what would my long-suffering neighbours say now? The red lights were more apparent in the foggy night than the scaffolding, anyone could make a mistake.

Next day a horde of men descended on me. They swarmed up the scaffolding like angry monkeys. No room for many weeks was sacred from their gaze. There were ear-splitting sounds of horrible ominous rumblings as they ripped and pulled the remaining tiles off the roof. One dashing energetic youth stood on a platform on the second storey madly shovelling rubble for eight hours a day whilst another boy stood on the ground directing passers-by in the lane to 'Watch out, missus', as over-zealousness on the part of the boy on the scaffolding sprayed rubble and dust on the passers-by. The general public watched with the mesmerized fascination which men digging holes in a road is apt to produce. Even today I swear that half Ringwood is suffering from wry necks as a result of the time when I had the roof retiled! The public really suffered terrible privation at this time; the weather was cold, there was danger from falling rubble, but they were tough. They stuck it out to the bitter end. They advised, they commented, they bet on the ultimate cost. They reminded each other of accidents that they had seen happen to other people mending other roofs in the High Street. Finally they bet the weather would break and the rain set in before the job was done. The general public worked really hard when my poor old roof was done; I don't think we could have achieved the ultimate result without their help. I never knew a market town with so many faithful adherents to the 'what-is-this-life-if-we-have-no-time-to-stand-and-stare' motif of living. I supposed it helped to pass the winter away.

From Monday until Thursday our men on the roof worked madly; if noise and mess was a criterion of good workmanship then these boys were pure gold medallists. Then on Thursday, at noon precisely, a strange unusual silence penetrated into the house. I found myself holding my breath, as I listened in vain for the now-usual sound of grating rubble, breaking glass or some such other noise to which my nervous system had by now become attuned. I was not mistaken; there was a silence like a tomb. Something was wrong. I know for certain that there was a great deal more glass to be broken. The energetic youth on the top floor was not likely to retire leaving anything whole behind him.

I decided to investigate, thinking that perhaps the four tilers had made a suicide pact and decided to end it all rather than face finishing the job which they declared every day to be 'a —— awful job, missus'. A few stragglers of the public were still waiting in the street below unable to believe that the performance for the moment was over.

I found the workmen having a conference in the shattered remains of what had once been my large glass-covered courtyard. The boy on the topmost piece of scaffolding had obviously been employed to hurl single tiles on to this glass roof. He hadn't had one miss. The cold January air flowed healthily into the court-yard—unrestricted.

'What's happened?' I said nervously.

'It's like this,' said the foreman. 'Unless we have more scaffolding on the side of the house we aren't going on with the job. It's too dangerous. We're going on strike until the architect has had another look at this place.'

I hated them violently at that moment. The foreman was a tough Irishman who meant what he said and had trained his assistants to shake their heads in assenting nods at his every word.

'Is *he* going too?' I asked faintly, pointing at the youngest member of the team who was the champion of glass-smashers. He'd seemed so happy in his job.

'Of course,' said the Irish foreman. 'When one goes we all go.' He ground his foot fiercely on to a cigarette, ignoring the inches of glass segments on which it rested.

'You'll come back?' I pleaded, although I hoped the youngster would be allowed to take his destructive poltergeist instincts elsewhere. After all, the roof of the courtyard had been all right until the glass-smasher had vented his spleen on it.

'That's as maybe,' said the foreman thoughtfully.

They went. All of them. Just like that, leaving the debris well distributed, ignored by them, as if it wasn't there at all.

I made signs from my window to the staring public in the road below that there would be no afternoon performance. They dispersed in orderly fashion but I knew that *they* at least would be back. After all, it isn't every day that you can see a roof sliding around in the High Street.

I have always used the glass-covered courtyard as an extra store-room. The night that the tilers went on strike it rained. Gleefully, the B.B.C. reported winds at gale force. What they didn't say was that some small demon had decided to concentrate most of the gale forces for miles around into one small area. To be precise, in my courtyard. That night I battled hard with elderly tarpaulin sheets to cover the furniture which was too big for me to move indoors. I was a Lilliputian in a land of forces too great for me. At 2 a.m. I gave up and condemned the lot to the elements. I have not the temperament to fight for too long against losing odds. The gale blew itself out. My garden fence was found some little way down the side lane, and there was about two feet of water in the courtyard. The mahogany furniture stored there had a strange, well-scrubbed appearance quite out of keeping with the original design.

I 'phoned my landlord.

The girl in the outer office put me through to the woman in the inner office who put me through to the secretary who handed me over to the managing director who finally located my landlord.

He was charming as usual. With my feet still wet from the paddling-pool in the courtyard I could feel the warmth of his over-heated innermost sanctum pervading over the telephone. Charming though he is, I hoped his roof would fall in one day. But nothing like that ever happens to landlords—only to tenants.

I told my landlord rather bluntly what had happened. He was quite disbelieving. He always says that I have too much imagination. I found myself actually shouting. After all, it is quite important to want to have a roof over one's head, it gives a person a sense of security.

My landlord promised quite sincerely to 'see into the matter'. As I rang off, I could imagine him solemnly telling the managing director to tell the secretary to tell the woman in the inner office to tell the girl at the switchboard in the outer office to ring the contracting builder to see to Mrs. Leek's roof. I sincerely hoped that the builder lived in a one-roomed bed-sitter with a single telephone permanently attached to his ear. If this was the case a little prompt action might occur. It's a far cry from a comfortable office in Bournemouth to a shop in the High Street in Ringwood, and my landlord is always such a busy man.

Later in the morning a neat businesslike figure arrived and approached the house. The architect had arrived. With great solemnity he climbed up the scaffolding. He lingered for one minute precisely on the roof, then descended to earth and disappeared in the direction of the car park. We never crossed words together but his swift journey heavenwards must have achieved some purpose, for the next day more scaffolding arrived. Finally the Irish foreman and his fellow poltergeists came back. I viewed the youth taking up his old position on the top storey with some dismay. I knew only too well what he had on his small mind! Now they really went to work. They ripped out the dormer windows and carpenters advanced in neat formations of twos. They bashed and sawed and finally fitted new window-frames, but they didn't bother with little nuisances like glass to begin with. After all, you know how healthy a cold January day can be. At night I huddled miserably around the fire in the lounge whilst a series of gale force winds, not anticipated by the B.B.C. 'Met' men, whipped the carpet practically from the floor. If the windows are not in tomorrow, I vowed with chattering teeth, I'll take to my bed and stay there, possibly I'll never get up again. Nobody cares at all for poor tenants like me.

Meanwhile the dust from the debris of the fragile roof invaded the house, filling every nook and cranny with fine sand-like deposits. I developed an attack of asthma which actually did drive me to my bed as I had prophesied. I lay there for three days not caring what the poltergeists were up to; from the constant noise I presumed that they were doing their worst.

Then I dragged myself wearily out of bed one morning to 'phone my landlord again. I wanted glass in those windows, or else! On this morning I reached only the outer office where a youthful voice informed me cheerfully that my landlord had 'gone to Switzerland on a vacation'.

This time I was savagely sincere in hoping that something quite dreadful would happen in his own home whilst he was away. I lay in bed seeing my landlord's new central-heating system which I knew he had had recently installed. Whilst he was merrily ski-ing in Switzerland, I hoped it would disintegrate. Alternatively I willed him to have left at least one tap flowing in his nice new house. I tried to calculate how many gallons of tap water would be needed to reduce his house to the same shambles that mine was in. Finally I destroyed his whole house and garages by a most devastating fire. Then I sank into a blissful sleep, united with my landlord in the throes of mutual complete and utter destruction.

Next morning I developed pleurisy! Every time the poltergeist builders threw a brick it seemed that it landed on my chest; I had great difficulty in breathing. I decided that the only thing to do was to die, and let *that* be a lesson to my cheerful landlord not to allow demon builders to do as they liked with any other tenant of his!

Suddenly, it was all over. I crawled from my bed into a great silence. Mysterious unknown hands had taken down the steel corset of the scaffolding whilst I had battled with the difficulties of breathing. The sun was shining as I tottered into the High Street feeling very fragile, but still alive.

I crossed the road and looked up at the roof. The new roof was indeed on, still slightly wavy but neat and intact with no signs of being able to slither again. The new dormers looked quite charming with the glittering blueness of fresh paint. Even the sudden realization that I should have to pay for this pleasant paint did not at that moment distract from the pleasure of looking at it.

It was over, this nightmare of demon builders and assistant poltergeists. I went indoors and switched on the radio; it would be wonderful to enjoy a programme at long last, free from interfering noises.

'Today is the first day of spring,' said the cultured voice on the B.B.C.

I couldn't believe it, but if the B.B.C. says its spring then spring it must be. They check their facts so thoroughly. I went upstairs to the top flat. I wanted to lean out of the window, the lovely new dormer windows. I wanted to gaze across the Bickerley to where the River Avon flows lazily towards Christchurch. I wanted to enjoy this first day of spring.

I entered the main bedroom, for it is from this window that one can get the best view of all. A large unsightly patch of torn-away laths and crumbled plaster greeted me, all round the new window-frames.

'But they've gone,' I said quite stupidly. 'The builders have gone and they've left all this unfinished.'

I tried to open the new casement; something was wrong. My fingers touched smooth new wood. The demon builders had forgotten to put a catch on the window!

My feet hardly touched the stairs as I dived for the 'phone. I asked for my landlord's number very firmly, I rudely dismissed the pleasantries of the outer and inner offices, I snorted past the secretary and the managing director.

I spoke to my landlord, I said a lot of words.

'Don't worry, my dear,' purred my landlord, 'they'll be back.'

I plunged the receiver back. It sounded like a threat to me.

From demon builders to poltergeists—Help!

3
Opening day
—a study in chaos

BY ANY known rule of business, this antique shop of ours in the High Street should never have survived the first month. We opened very, very quietly—no brilliant cocktail party; no local big names to wish us success; indeed, the now-almost-forgotten date of opening was rather shrouded in gloom. Our first visitor was a rather doleful elderly lady. She drifted into the shop and morbidly eyed the contents as well as me with, at first, suspicion and then with a distinctly morose balefulness.

'Think you'll do well here?' she asked.

'Well, it is early to tell yet, but I hope so.'

'Can't see it myself—lot of these shops about, no one buys this here old-fashioned stuff now.' (This was in a slightly more cheerful tone as if the vision of my ultimate downfall really afforded her some crumb of happiness.)

The conversation was one which would ultimately kill my normal optimistic spirit and I could see no future in replying, so I dusted madly with a dangerous flourish of my feather duster.

'I give you a month,' croaked this spirit of joy.

This really was too much.

'Perhaps I'll make so much money in a month that I'll retire,' I replied in quite my most testy voice.

I think she saw that I was becoming cross, for now she changed her mode of attack a little. 'Well, I don't see anything here that I want today.' Then, threateningly, 'But I'll call again to see how you are getting on.'

I was reduced to muttering.

My second customer entered delicately—a hesitant touch on the door which did not open as easily as it should (memo: see to that tomorrow!), so I grabbed the handle from the inside to help her and pulled too hard. Enter a lady with great rapidity; true, I caught her before she actually hit the floor but it was not an auspicious beginning. The lady was nervous, and I was unnerved. Still, I hand it to her, she was game. Once in the shop she moved round, slightly gingerly at first for the original floorboards were still under the tenancy of incipient dry rot, but gradually we both gained confidence.

The lady apparently was interested in Staffordshire figures, of which I had perhaps a dozen placed at strategic points in the window. We had them all out and spent a long time assessing their virtue and value. By now I was sure that the lady was to be my very first customer, the first person to cross my hand with silver in the new shop. She liked two figures and did not faint at the price and finally paid for them. Although delighted with this gesture, I suddenly went very hot around the neck. In the whole of the shop I hadn't a single sheet of wrapping-paper! You simply cannot throw Staffordshire figures into a shopping-bag. A brilliant idea took me by storm. I dived into my neighbour's shop and borrowed two sheets of paper. Triumphantly I wrapped the figures in the borrowed paper and then I became aware for the very first time of *it*. This is the exact moment when I first noticed the aroma of fish, for my neighbouring shop is occupied by a fishmonger. Quickly I gave the figures to the lady and saw her to the door, then I sat down to concentrate on what during the years has been at first a problem and worry and finally a great joke amongst my friends—how to win the battle against the smell of fish. It seeps into the shop in great waves; it clings on to lace and fabrics, and, like the poor, it is for ever with me. At this early period even my best friends didn't really want to know me and I know that even the kindest of them were sceptical about the lasting-power of the shop. In my most logical of moods I face the fact that really we should *not* have become a success, for we had none of the basic ingredients unless it was a never-dying hope in my heart. The smell of fish in this first month almost submerged me but in the end the only thing to do was to treat it as a joke.

When my more fastidious customers enter with lace handkerchiefs delicately arranged over their aquiline noses I never fail to throw out some bright crack. If I can only *talk* quickly enough I can divert their minds from the smell, at least sufficiently long to do some business. I bought about a hundred sprays, all guaranteed to help in the battle against smell. I bought strong-smelling flowers and herbs, scents and potions with aromatic virtue, but I have news for the manufacturers of some very famous branded goods. Your products didn't do a thing! In the battle for the nose the fish wins fins down, not once but consistently.

My neighbours are the nicest of people, fantastically clean and always willing to be helpful, so even though we have a constant '*smell*' with us and between us we have always lived in a neighbourly fashion. I don't think we have had a cross word in all the years we have been here. It helps a lot to have nice neighbours when you have a shop in the High Street.

During the first week here I heard fourteen prognostications of 'They won't last long'; ten rather unoriginal remarks of 'I give them a month'; twenty-two local prophets, however, plumped for the fact that our disaster would be 'Shops with a side entrance aren't much good in a High Street'.

Yes, we have *that* too—all modern inconveniences and disadvantages are in this shop, for we have a fairly high step from the footpath into a little porch-like arrangement. From this porch you can go right, into the fish shop, or left, into the antique shop. We also have a dip in the floor as you reach the door and then there is a last obstacle of a one-inch-high piece of weatherboard. Apart from a trip-wire, I can think of nothing that we have missed to *prevent* customers entering the shop!

Having possessed the stamina actually to arrive in the shop, we have so much stuff packed into the place that it is far wiser for the customer to remain in a state of suspended animation, breathing as little as possible, whilst we try to do business. Miraculously we have survived. Our regular customers now bound through the preliminary obstacle-course with the fitness of Olympic athletes; they avoid head-on collisions with cases of stuffed birds; they zigzag over the floor with a hiccupping cha-cha-like dexterity of movement; and they *buy*. Out go the stuffed birds, the Dresden candelabra, the silver and the plate, the pictures, bronze figures, the Chinese household gods and the Buddhas. In comes the same old smell of fish for its daily duel with the joss-sticks burnt in front of the Buddhas. In come the new goods; every day we buy just as every day we sell. The accumulation of years makes a startling, eye-catching sight in a shop that never has a dull moment.

On opening day in that far-away month of April we had a load of hope, very little money and a quaint old accumulation of goods, and in the middle of all this there was always a tiny new fear; a fear that *perhaps* the smell of fish would prove too much; a fear that perhaps the customers would not like the shop; a fear that our tiny, so-insignificant bit of capital would fade away and, behind it all, a fear of being a failure.

But by May not one of these fears remained; they died natural deaths. How did I live through that opening day? After the episode of the 'no wrapping-paper' there was the rather more sad episode of the *mice*. This shop in the High Street was originally a bread and cake shop. When we had been working at nights to get the shop ready to open we often had the assistance of numerous minute scurrying furry bodies, desperately hoping to find a crumb here or a morsel of cake there. Although I hate destroying anything, it was obvious that woodworm, mice, the smell of fish and antiques could not live in happy co-existence. Something had to give! So—over to the corn shop across the road to find some lethal weapon with which to combat the mice. The contents of sundry tins were strewn around the shop according to the instructions on the labels.

On opening day I had forgotten these tins and indeed I had forgotten the mice, until a customer in the afternoon decided to explore the regions at the extreme back of the shop. I moved with her towards the object which she desired to examine. Wishing to play the part of an efficient, courteous and most willing assistant (the pride and joy of any shop), I bent down to pick up a brass bowl. To my horror, inside the bowl I saw two tiny and very, very sad, stiff, little furry figures of mice! With a brilliant sleight of hand which would have done credit to Canasta himself I palmed the furry little twins and handed the bowl to my customer. Madam examined the bowl and decided to buy it. Now I was faced with what to do with the mice whilst wrapping the bowl and still giving Madam my full attention. In one easy movement I twisted my handkerchief round them and thrust the whole thing —twin mice and handkerchief—into the neck of my dress. Squeamishness is a foreign part of my nature but the excitement of the day plus the faintest touch of those miserable little bodies against my chest almost made me sick.

Madam was precipitated to the door with great rapidity and then the mice were removed and consigned to the waste-paper basket. But the day was not yet ended. Behind the desk at the back of the shop was a veritable slaughter-house of mice, a massacre indeed had taken place. Sadly I got the dustpan and swept the tight little bodies into it, wrapped them in a new copy of the *Lady* and buried them with the twins in the depths of the waste-paper basket. Death for a crumb of bread! Even the stuffed birds were better off than delinquent mice in a new antique shop.

At the end of our first day I had taken seventeen pounds. It was the most thrilling seventeen pounds I have ever handled.

The next day, no one came into the shop at all—and that is how it is in an antique shop. One day a fortune can come into your hands, the next day you may have difficulty in changing a pound note, but it is never lacking in interest, never dull. The goods you handle tell their own story of adventure, and an antique shop draws people from all walks of life—the surest magnet for meeting interesting personalities. Each day you learn a little more, and although you live amongst the bygones of the past they are given new life by the present-day people who come into the shop and ultimately buy them. It is the nicest possible way to learn history!

From that first chaotic day in a sun-spangled month of April, almost a lifetime ago, I have loved every minute of being in this shop in the High Street.

4

A little something
for over the fireplace

T HEY entered the shop with the velocity of a minor whirlwind. A delightful, very English family, bringing with them a breath of elegance associated with Bond Street on the part of the ladies. The men had just the right manly tang of tweed and tobacco which one connects with the true type of almost blue-blooded Englishmen. The mother, elegant, young in spirit and looks, a carefully maintained lady who would always evoke the most normal of love from her husband and the dutiful respect of her offspring. The children, products of the best private schools and now about to go up to one of the universities. The husband, every inch a family man, contented and happy as the pearl in the bosom of his well-brought-up family, a veritable breadwinner.

As they enter the door I smell the peculiar tingling scent of money. At first it is exhilarating, for this is a challenge—how to do the magician's act of transferring paper money from their leather wallets into the coldness of my cashbox? How, most of all, to achieve this in an easy movement, for the advent of a family in a small shop presents problems, one is unable to give the dominant party all one's consideration. In the middle of a bewitching sales talk, Elder Brother will swoop on to a collection of medals; with war-whoops of delight he will insist on diverting the attention of Mother and Father from the main idea, i.e. to purchase something! At the sight of the medals Father is moved into an eulogy of reminiscences ranging from 'ones he has got at home' to 'Do you remember Great-Uncle Toby, how proud he was of the M.C. which he won at so and so'. This can go on for hours, for mention of Uncle Toby brings forth a little small talk about his spouse, dear Aunt Margaret, who could not *bear* native work of any kind. The sight of a carved Indian table apparently had been known to send her into hysterics, yes, really!

Just as you are drawing breath to go back into the attack, little sister Sue sees the case of jewellery; gasps of girlish delight as she plucks rings from cards willy-nilly. Inevitably, one becomes jammed and the usual titter of laughter followed by the squeak of, 'Oh, Mummy, *now* I'll *have* to buy it.'

Alas, the jewellery stirs up other patent memories of the jewellery that the burglar took: all the best-regulated families speak with pride of past burglaries. This year, if you haven't had a burglary you are definitely *passé* and most certainly non-U.

By now you are desperate. Already you have forgotten what it was you were trying to sell them, and suddenly the money which you might have had doesn't matter. All you want is a peaceful shop or perhaps just one tiny timid little customer who only wants to spend five shillings on a birthday present.

Miraculously, Father now calls his brood to attention sheepishly, but nevertheless effectively. True, the box of medals are overthrown in a valiant attempt to achieve order, but it is a bagatelle. For good measure Little Sister lunges at the rows of necklaces in the corner and is innocently happy trying to strangle herself, doing a Bea Lillie act of swinging a jet necklace round and round her throat. Being quite beastly, you hope she succeeds. One corpse would not matter! Mother now has become practical. At last you elicit that she has really come to buy a little something for over the fireplace. Vaguely, with much flapping of pearly tipped manicured hands, she indicates size—generally the entire room is involved in this action. You mentally divide it by half and take away the number you first thought of. Has Madam any idea of the type of picture she wants: a landscape, a still life, a flower piece or even a portrait? After all, there is a wealth of subject matter involved in the make-up of a picture. Triumphantly Madam announces that she would adore a picture of a *horse*. By this time she has cast a crafty eye around and discovered that the only horsey picture you have is way, way out of reach and it needs a major Olympic type of manœuvre to capture it. To produce it whole and still be in one piece yourself should logically mean that you sell the picture. Do not delude yourself. Madam and family have the whole afternoon to devote to this pursuit of finding a little something for over the fireplace. A few broken pots, your laddered stockings and a marked shortness of breath are not going to put them off. She is now warming up. The horse picture is nice but don't you think he is a bit sad-looking for a horse, not at all like Giblets, the children's pony? Now off we go at a canter on the subject of how intelligent poor old Giblets was, and the last straw of all we get the sad, sad story of how poor old Giblets died. The shop is saved from being submerged in a flood of tears only by the boys seeing a collection of battleaxes, knives and swords. Giblets is forgotten; they fling themselves on the swords and prepare to do an Errol Flynn act on the stairs. Almost you long to retrieve the subject of Giblets, at least the flow of tears would be peaceful whilst the clash of swords sets your teeth on edge.

Mother has now quite lost interest in the horse picture and is pondering on a set of miniatures whilst murmuring aloud, 'Did Darling think she should buy them or wait for Aunt Tabby to die when she would inherit her lovely set of miniatures.' 'Darling' by now is becoming bored; the sight of decanters reminds him that soon he will be wanting a drink and he decides to rush matters. Children are gathered, the party counted only to discover that little sister Sue is not one of us. In the shindigeree of the Errol Flynn act she has wandered into the book store on the second floor and after many calls she emerges clutching a volume of poetry. Wait for it—she just adores Shelley!

An indulgent father pays a shilling for Shelley, hurrah for Shelley! It is a small triumph but for one hour's work you now have a credit of one shilling. (You pay your charwoman three shillings an hour whilst you earn a shilling!)

Madame La Mère is now taking the centre of the floor and is

obviously about to give birth to a bright idea. 'Darling,' she says, 'I think perhaps we should *not* have a picture. After all, we have *one* picture already. . . .'

Darling responds magnificently. 'Of course we have, I'd forgotten.'

'Darling,' she says, 'I think I shall buy a mirror. Perhaps you could show us a nice mirror about this' (again the world-embracing gesture) 'size.'

I have about twenty mirrors scattered over the house. A quick mental recap says if I show her all the mirrors and she spends only two minutes looking at each one she will be here for another forty minutes. Perish the thought!

My mind now becomes made up. Maliciously I remember a particularly revolting abortion of a mirror which we hid in the back room months ago. I resolve to show this to her and so get rid of them for ever. Even not to take any money now becomes preferable to another forty minutes with this family; in forty minutes those boys could have discovered the stamp collection or the model cars and then, heaven help us all!

I pull and grunt and produce it—the mirror that should never have been born. It's old and has every bad feature about it, the shape is wrong, the glass is foxed and it is pseudo and a bastard to any known period of history.

Forcing back a shudder I display it and wait for the reaction.

'But, dar . . ling . . . it's the *very* thing, just what I've always wanted; it will look marvellous, just the thing for over the fireplace.'

I am too shattered and nerve-racked to follow up with any line of sales talk, the whole affair has become a matter of fate and quite out of my hands. In a daze I find paper and string, I hand it to them. With shaking hands I put the money—real money too—in the till, I drag the door open and they troop out flashing bright smiles of love and appreciation at each other as they move into the street.

All that remains of a nightmare is the smell of 'Darling's' pipe-tobacco and a *débâcle* of ruins: a mountain of swords to be put away; a picture lightly tossed into a seat; the medals on the floor (My God, they *did* find the stamps!). I pick up the picture of the horse and almost I could believe that he winks at me. Gently I replace him on the wall, for we have now shared an experience, a thing of great moment, and there is a quietness in us.

It's all so like bashing your head against a wall; so very, very pleasant when you stop. Ah well, that's the selling business.

After all, they only wanted a little something for over the fireplace! No harm in *that*, is there?

5
Art—for money's sake

THERE is nothing more difficult to understand than art and its connections with an antique shop. The buying and selling of pictures can come under the heading of Big Business. Customers today no longer look for just a pretty picture to put on the wall. Today they want *art*. That means a picture that is a financial investment, and even the most minute purchase must be classified, pedigreed and authenticated before the client is completely happy. Unfortunately the whole world seems to dream of finding an old master for a song. In the distant recesses of their mind they can always remember Uncle William who once bought a genuine Renoir at a jumble sale for sixpence. Art has become a sticky wicket for the antique dealer and because of the contact that we have with Art circles we are more aware of the traps and disappointments in buying pictures. Because of this dream the antique shops nowadays have gained another section of the public, all madly art-conscious, all madly seeking to fulfil the dream of finding a famous picture that will command a high price.

A pile of elderly looking canvases stacked nonchalantly in the corner of the shop with their faces turned to the wall are a certain magnet which never fails to attract the hungry art-hunting fraternity. People from all walks of life seem to be ready to join in the hunt. Passers-by arrive to go through the stack, untidily but avidly. Mildly I always ask if they are looking for anything in particular, this way I could save them a lot of trouble. But is it trouble, perhaps it is pleasure as well, and who am I to spoil anyone's pleasure?

'Oh no,' they say, and if they are hunting in couples they give each other meaning looks and often a nudge or two for good measure. 'We would rather look for ourselves.'

I get the message from their looks that I am not wanted and retire to do some work in the shop such as pricing up other stock.

The casual hunting types fall for anything featuring flowers, whilst portraits cause mirth and landscapes are apt to be passed over.

However, I have one customer who used to come regularly every month and declare every landscape that she found to be 'Constable'. The utterance was always given in the tones of the utmost assurance. It was a statement which I scarcely dared to deny. She was an impressive, dominant character and like a certain historical character who had 'Calais' engraved on her heart, this customer had 'Constable' on her mind. One day I put an ultra-modern landscape at the bottom of my pile of canvases and waited for the inevitable delighted cry of 'Constable'. This time the word came out almost in the form of a question. 'Constable . . .?' I solemnly agreed that it was unusual for Constable to paint a local scene in only two shades of colour. Particularly as in this case only the most brilliant pillar-box red and acid green had been used. It was a truly modern painting!

After this episode my customer seemed to lose faith in my pile of canvas, perhaps the local landscape broke her heart. Anyway, I haven't seen the lady for four months but I am quite sure that she has not given up her search for landscapes.

Once I sold her a small Morland, but even when I impressed it on her that it was indeed a Morland she gave me a look implying that she knew better. Not even a receipt stating clearly that she had bought a Morland daunted her, but she was happy with the picture. A 'rose by any other name' was applicable in this case.

After the casual passers-by, enter the dealers, generally the scouts for the big London galleries. They call every time they are in the vicinity and are on a full-time job of scouring the little shops in the West Country. These are the big-game hunters of the picture world. They know exactly what they are looking for. They are very willing to buy anything. Anything, that is, that would not be out of place in the National Gallery! Of course, the price must be 'right'. This means that if I am ignorant enough to have anything good enough for them they will 'take it off my hands'. I find the big-game-hunting types rather wearisome. They are insistent in looking through every canvas in the shop and always aim to get into my back room, where very often I have put something interesting on one side for one of my favourite dealers. Lately whenever one of the scouts for the big galleries comes into the shop I just say, 'The Renoirs are in the cellar, the Picassos in the top flat, the El Grecos need cleaning and we have sold right out of Dutch still-life this week. . . .'

It clears the air quite a lot. So much time is wasted by people hoping to find the sublime amongst the ridiculous. Sometimes I suppose it must happen but I hope I have never so lacked in sense as to sell a picture of rare value for a mere song.

Actually, I suppose I can can say that I have had a fairly good training in art. I must freely admit that I have made many mistakes, but as I get older I hope that I do not make so many. After all, what is the use of gaining experience if I do not profit from past mistakes? Life would be just a waste of time. Since my childhood I have been lucky enough to have met many contemporary artists. I have also had the privilege of being able to find time to travel, and during this time I have browsed around the famous galleries of the Continent as well as the London galleries. I suppose I have learnt more from hours spent in the Louvre than anywhere else. Even so, there is so much to be learnt every day. My good friend Cecil has been wonderful in teaching me much about pictures. From him I learnt about tempera painting, but more important was that he taught me to recognize that elusive thing called 'quality'. The mysterious 'something' which I cannot describe but, miraculously, I can now recognize. Possibly the secret for successful buying and selling of pictures is to be able to recognize that it is well painted, irrespective of subject or signature. If a good horse can't be of a bad colour, then a good picture cannot be badly painted. A picture with the paint worked thinly over the canvas will never clean and it is a waste of time to dream that it will ever have any high value.

I have never had any spectacular finds in pictures, nothing to take my breath away. On the other hand I have bought numerous paintings that have turned out better on examination and have made a steady profit. I rarely rush to sell a painting. In antiques such as furniture and jewellery I have always been happy to take a quick profit and turn over the money I have laid out. This policy cannot be carried through to paintings. It is far better to think about them, even to sit quietly looking at them and then to check and compare with other pictures of the same school. It pays good dividends in the long run.

Cecil, bless his heart, had a spectacular flair for finding the right pictures and apart from playing a few tricks on me he has always been helpful in placing a picture with the right client at a sensible price. We have had some good deals together in pictures. Cecil is himself a very fine artist and is a wonderful man on restoration. He likes to guard his secrets in this line of the business as carefully as a miser guards his stocking-leg. Once he deliberately gave me the wrong ingredient for cleaning a picture. Actually, there was no real harm done, the picture was of little value and any lesson in art has to be a hard one. It taught me a lesson. Look out for pictures but mind my own business in connection with cleaning! I keep this picture to remind me that no one should strain any friendship by nosing into someone else's trade secrets. Now I am quite happy just to buy and sell.

One day I received the catalogue for a big house sale. On the day of the viewing I was more interested in the furniture than in the pictures. Just as I was about to leave I saw a very large canvas at the end of a room that I had not bothered to visit. It was the end of the day, the electricity had been cut off and the torch I always carry was on its last legs. Try as I would, I could not distinguish anything except a large black mass on the canvas although my fingers told me that the frame was magnificently carved in wood. When I got home I studied the catalogue but it gave no other details than the lot number and that it was 'Portrait of a Young Man' in carved frame and the size.

I was determined to buy the picture to get the frame, which I could imagine very well as a mirror.

On the day of the sale the weather was fine enough for the auction to be held on the lawn. This meant that only the smaller items were brought out to be displayed. The lot number of the picture was called but of course it was not displayed. Bidding started at twenty guineas and went up quickly to forty-five. There was a lull and I thought I had made the last bid. Then I saw the auctioneer was looking towards the opposite side of the lawn to where I was standing. I made frantic signs and caught his eye in the nick of time. The Bournemouth dealer had turned away at fifty guineas and I became the owner of a 'Young Man'. I decided to take the picture with me that night. It was an unco-operative type of picture and difficult to load on to the roof of the car. Just as we reached the shop the heavens opened and there was a cloudburst. No picture has ever been unloaded so roughly but we got it in the porch of the shop before the rain touched it.

It was the sort of picture never meant to go through anything so banal as a shop door. This picture had been painted for a mansion and it was prepared to fight back for its rights. We ended up by taking the door of the shop off its hinges before it would condescend to being trundled in. We were very wet, very tired and very cross. The picture was immaculate, gazing at us with imperturbable eyes.

The canvas proved to be a glorious surprise. True it was dirty but, after cleaning, the black coat of the Young Man turned out to be dark green. As the cleaning process went on I became more interested in the Young Man, and less intrigued with the frame. Finally I sold the picture for two hundred and fifty pounds and kept the frame. When I had converted it into a mirror I got back the initital cost of fifty guineas. It was a successful adventure into pictures.

For a week I went round with my head in the clouds and

suffered from such delusions of grandeur that I even toyed with the idea of changing the name of the shop in the High Street to some high-faluting name like 'Avon Galleries'. A glance at some awful canvases which would live with me for ever as a series of mistakes brought me back to earth with a bump and saved me the cost of a new sign over the window.

It had been too easy and I had had luck running well with me. With something approaching humility I finally invested some of the easy-earned cash in two pictures painted by Cecil. It seemed to be an act of justice to plough back some money into the works of a living artist and I have had the utmost joy from his two small paintings. Quite frankly I would have hated to have lived for too long with the 'Portrait of a Young Man': he was not my type at all. Even when he was clean and shining, his expression has remained mournful. As I type this I can look at Cecil's pictures and feel sheer joy in owning them.

This shop of mine has always attracted more than the normal quota of bearded-weirdies and all with pronounced artistic tendencies. The New Forest lures artists to its bosom and gradually they find their way to the shop. It gives the house part of the place a somewhat unexpected Left Bank look. All artists who have been here have left behind something of themselves. I have probably the only bathroom and lavatory with personal mural motifs on the walls! My top flat has been a resting place for so many artists, generally in their penniless days. Often I have sold paintings just in the nick of time to keep the local bailiff at bay and enabled the artist to buy paint and canvas for yet another potential masterpiece. I look back on my wandering artists with great tenderness and when some of them make the grade and hold a successful exhibition, it has been more of a thrill to me than if I had actually found an old master. Some remember this place but, because they are human, some forget. For me there will always be the happiest of memories from a group of people who can make me forget the humdrum life of a mere shopkeeper. People like Ben Segal, now a well-known sculptor in America, who first introduced me to the unexpected finer points of abstract painting. It was like entering into a new world to hear Ben talk, and heavens how we talked!

The modern artist is a wonderful person; he knows so much and knows just how far the chosen medium of his art will take him. I admire his sense of dedication. Today the artist has a place in the world: the public no longer looks askance at him and condemns him as mad. The difference that I see now that I am in my forties and able to make comparisons with artists of two generations is that the present-day artist knows just how to sell his work to the best advantage. This is a good omen. I have never believed that art should be a thing apart or that artists must suffer in order to paint well. Most of my artists have done far better work on a reasonable amount of food and a few glasses of good wine. Art is a good business today and none the worse for this, I feel.

The saddest thing in picture-hunting is to find a picture that one knows to be 'right' and be unable to buy it for lack of the necessary money. It is even worse if one has a genuine affection for the same picture.

Early in 1960 I went to a sale in a house in nearby Bournemouth. The catalogue was devoted almost entirely to paintings and prints. I knew practically everything offered for sale, as I had known the deceased owner. I entered the marquee on the day of the sale to find that every major gallery in London had sent along a representative. It was a fantastic array of famous faces, a rural edition of Sotheby's.

Every picture made a wonderful price. I could almost hear the executors rubbing their hands as each price lengthened favourably. I knew that the *pièce de résistance* would be a very fine small flower-painting by the Dutch Van Aast. I had admired this painting when I had visited the house and resolved that I would 'go for it'. There were many interesting pictures before the Van Aast but I did not dare to bid for them as I had to reserve my finances for this major work. It was a picture to love, rich with age and superbly executed. The last Van Aast that I had seen was in a London gallery and priced at eight hundred pounds. At that time the price had made me wince, but on this particular day at the sale I was in a better financial position to buy. How stupid can one be? As the Van Aast was brought in, not even the dim light of the marquee could eliminate the glory of the work although it seemed smaller than I remembered it to be. The first glimpse of it sent a rustle of anticipation amongst the whole assembly. I would not have been surprised if everyone had risen to their feet as a token of respect. There was this terrific electrifying feeling and then by contrast—complete silence.

The auctioneer did not waste time, he had obviously got several bids 'on the book' for it. He started at five hundred pounds and I noticed with approval that it was a member of the public who started the bidding. The London dealers sat mute; one studied his feet, another read the catalogue as if he were afraid to miss some vital piece of information in it. Another pair sat at a grotesque angle under a palm tree solemnly consulting watches and fidgeting as if they were impatient. Almost like a general viewing the landscape for possible enemies, I watched and waited. I remember thinking that the danger would come from the potted-palm area. Those two dealers were too disinterested but I recognized one as the agent for a famous dealer whose name is known all over the world. Suddenly at a thousand pounds I threw in a bid by a defiant wave of a purple glove. The auctioneer eyed me approvingly as if he enjoyed the idea of new blood entering the fighting arena.

The members of the public gradually dropped out as the bidding rose. There was no hurry, but every bid was decisive. I had never wanted anything so much as I wanted that picture. I forgot the image of my bank balance as I remembered that nearly all Dutch still-life paintings are liable to fetch fantastic prices. At two thousand five hundred pounds I was punch-drunk.

And still in the bidding although I had a moment when I saw myself for a moment actually being the purchaser of the picture, and possibly facing a divorce from my husband for daring to buy it. Can one get a divorce because a wife spends every penny in the kitty on a picture? At three thousand pounds I had mentally borrowed some extra money from a relation of mine by promising to go halves on the picture.

Thirty seconds later I was myself again but it was a mad, glorious moment whilst it lasted. The picture was worth every penny and even if I had had to pay out the three thousand pounds for it I think I would have been very happy.

Alas, the bidding went on, and on, and on. It resolved into a silent battle between the palm tree and the chaise-longue. I bet myself half a crown on the palm tree standing the siege, but it was no satisfaction to win. I watched the glorious little painted panel carried to the men under the palm tree, a brief moment of consultation with the porter, a gathering of briefcases and they were gone. Two dealers and a picture; a small part of me suffered the pangs of death as the Van Aast disappeared down the path. I can remember even now that I thought 'this is the sort of picture I could easily steal' and was horrified at the idea. That is the way a picture can get you. There is no escape when you fall in love with a picture and it is like unrequited love when the realization hits you that you will never see it again. In no other branch of antiques is a little knowledge so dangerous a thing. It breeds jealousy and desire and can bring on a touch of madness that taints one for ever.

I dreamt about the Van Aast for many nights. It took a lot of hard routine work to get it out of my system. Even now when the memory of that small painted panel of flowers floats in front of my eyes my heart lurches, and I feel sick when I think that only money stopped it from being mine.

Money. The awful limitation to owning something that I would have wanted to keep for ever, to own and to enjoy.

In pictures I know I am apt to become slightly abnormal, but I also know that if I could follow my instinct I have the right feeling to buy pictures which could become a famous collection. I have never really wanted to own anything else except the Van Aast and it is one of the times I hated being a shopkeeper.

Sometimes I wish I could look at a picture and see nothing. Yet I still dream of being able to buy something like the Van

Aast and of being able to keep it. I realize it is a dream, but there is no law against an antique dealer having dreams beyond her financial station.

The real tragedy of having learnt just a little about paintings is that I no longer enjoy a visit to the National Gallery as I used to do. To look is not enough, there is always the desire to own the painting. The tantalizing thrill of being able to say: 'This is mine. I'll let you share in the enjoyment of it but I won't sell it.'

I no longer want to have reproductions of famous pictures on my walls, it must be the real thing or nothing, yet years ago there was a thrill in a cheap reproduction of a Van Gogh. I saved up to buy a print of his 'Man in a Yellow Straw Hat' when I was ten. My mother still has it. Sometimes when I look at it on the staircase of my mother's house I stop for a moment. He started this lifelong hunting-for-pictures gamble and yet I have no feelings for him.

At the moment I have thirteen pictures forming the nucleus of a very modest private collection but each one gives me a thrill of pleasure every time I look at it.

I remind myself that I must be thankful for small mercies. Strangely enough, I have never in all my life had any desire to paint!

I have to face facts. I am just a hard-working ordinary type who happens to own an antique shop. I did not marry an oil magnate and I am never likely to inherit money or win a football pool. No matter if I work twenty-four hours a day for the rest of my life, I know I will never be able to harness my taste in pictures to the state of my pocket.

In the meantime I hope that thirteen is not my unlucky number. One day I must buy number fourteen. Better be on the safe side.

6
My grandmother
thought a lot about these . . .

HAVE you ever considered the fact that most antique dealers have a mournful visage and are often much younger in actual years than they appear to be by the look on their faces? Possibly the reason is to be found in the fact that every day they suffer the pangs of a great disillusionment. The feeling is very much akin to falling out of love; the beauty and virtues of the loved ones of yesterday, today are no longer apparent. The ultimate fulfilment is not to be—constant water wears away stone and constant disillusion destroys the antique dealer.

If one could pick and choose, to buy only the finest, rarest, most lovely things, how easy would be the lot of the dealer! Instead, he must search through a lot of dross to find one tiny glitter of gold. Numerous people call at the shop and say, 'I wonder if you would be interested in buying a few things that I want to sell?' My own appointment-book is always full for three weeks ahead for calls which I have to make. Tactfully I try to find out just what the lady has for sale but she is coy and can only murmur about 'a few things belonging to my grandma. . . .' A rapid calculation of the lady's age brings you to surmise that grandma was probably a Victorian so there is hope that amongst the little somethings there may be a morsel of interest. You press the enquiries—any glass (preferably coloured), any silver, or even plate, etc., etc. With a maddeningly gay little laugh milady says 'Oh, there's *masses* of everything—glass, silver and plate, funny little boxes, etc., etc.' The prospect visibly brightens.

Cancel the date you had made for a dinner party, for almost certainly that is the only date the client has available for you to call. Take down the address methodically, try to pinpoint the exact location of the house and do not, I beg of you, be fobbed off with 'Oh, *everybody* knows the house', for that has been my downfall many, many times. It is a great myth that other people know where you live. They don't; and you can spend hours of time, an extra gallon of petrol and be quite devoid of patience when you finally run your client to earth. She neglected to tell you that the short cut she mentioned led you across a ploughed field and to a railway crossing which had the gates shut after 6 p.m.!

Still you made it, but you feel by now that if there is a plum to be had in this house it will be a miracle and by heaven you certainly deserve it! If your client lives in Burley you are almost certain to be shown into the lounge and offered a glass of reasonably good sherry. You enter the lounge and your heart beats a little quicker for the sherry is in a Georgian decanter on a silver salver. The table on which it rests is a fine one and all around the room are visible signs of good taste and investments in the shape of fine porcelain, or a 'right' picture. You are deluded into a sense of well-being, mentally you toast the deceased grandma as you sip the sherry and you are burning with a curiosity to see the little treasures about which she thought so much. In your eagerness to do this you almost choke on the last drop of sherry, indicating that now you are ready to do business.

Gracefully you ask if perhaps anything in the present room is for sale, although in your heart you know it is not likely to be so. Still, you may as well try since you are here!

Now you move in brisk procession into another room where the treasures of the unknown grandmother are to be paraded for your inspection. As soon as you enter you realize that Grandma must have had some very odd moments in her life. Surely the same person who bought the *famille-rose* bowl in the other room could not have bought the garish Japanese tea-service. No, no, she had an enemy who gave it to her for a present! That must be the explanation. Then your eyes take in all the rest of the stuff and you realize that either Grandma had many, many enemies all determined to give her ghastly presents or that she had more moments of bad taste than her descendants dreamt of. There is certainly coloured glass—*thick, moulded stuff*—and the 'silver' is conspicuous by its absence until you spot a battered dressing-case with glass jars; each one has a minute quantity of silver on it, heavily monogrammed of course. The plate is all E.P.N.S. and quite the nastiest designs you have seen since you last went to a church bazaar.

It is a sad, sad moment for everyone. *You* want to buy and have the money to pay for it, your client wants to sell, but what can be the ultimate end for stuff of this quality? Your client prattles on, so far impervious to the fact that you are liable to have an attack of apoplexy at any moment. She picks up the revolting crude Jap tea-service and points out that 'Grandma thought a lot about her things. See, after all these years, not a chip or a haircrack anywhere.' Savagely you have visions of dear Grandma hiding the tea-service in a dark, dark cupboard and resolutely forgetting it; that is the only reason that it could have escaped the fact of a chip or haircrack.

Bitterly you think of the *famille-rose* bowl in the other room and then your hostess pounces and you know that this is the moment when you cease to be friends, for now you are invited to make an offer for the lot. Almost gently you point out that it is not quite the type of stuff you expected to see; that the plate is purely E.P.N.S., but since you have taken the trouble to make the journey you are prepared to offer x pounds for the whole lot. Now you retreat behind the heaviest piece of furniture and await the barrage of remarks which almost always follow. 'Do you really think I would sell all this?' (A vast all-taking-in wave of the hand). 'I'd sooner give it away.' This of course is a rank lie; had she wished to give it away she would have done so long ago, but the people with money don't give things away except perhaps in lieu of services rendered. This of course is how you earn the name for being a 'hard woman to deal with'. The good prices you have given for past things are never mentioned, only the poor prices you have offered for the things which 'my grandma thought a lot about'. It is a sad moment, this one of disillusionment; sad because the warmth of the sherry, the momentary taking into the family bosom, is now a thing of the past. You are an enemy, a viper in the bosom of the family; you are out to steal their heritage, their mess of pottage. You, on your part—remembering the cancelled dinner party, the long weary trek into the country and the utter despondency at seeing this load of rubbish—you are now wanting only to get home. With or without the rubbish is incidental. Tiredness and disappointment almost make you rude; after all, there is no law that demands that you must stay and listen whilst someone implies that you are trying to obtain things for nothing.

It is a waste of both breath and time to argue, although a faint semblance of courtesy makes you listen, whilst your client burbles irately that years ago a well-known, reputable dealer had offered her fifty pounds for this stuff. The intonation of 'reputable' is intended to be a nasty rub at you, rather implying that you don't know your business. In the early days of dealing these remarks are apt to make you touchy, but as time goes on you learn to shrug your shoulders. In your own mind the art of dealing is crystal clear. There are some things which all the world and his wife are looking for; these things you can give as good a price for as the next man. All you need is a good spy system for tracking them down. Everyone has exaggerated ideas of the value of their grandmother's possessions and, to be brutal, more ancestors had poor taste than is realized.

For my part I never haggle. If the articles offered to me are not of the type which I am seeking I put a price on them and that is it, resisting all encouragement to raise the bid by another halfpenny. If I am doomed to have a load of 'bad stock' then I must have it at a price that means I can stick it in a back room and forget it for a few months until a chance buyer may want to nibble at a single item.

Incidents such as the lady trying to sell the Jap tea-service are everyday affairs—one leaves most houses a little more despondent every time and certainly feeling many years older. With every 'bad' buy a little more of your reputation is left behind. Multiply the incident of the Jap tea-service fifty times in one month and you have an adequate reason for all antique dealers looking old before their time.

Only recently I had an enquiry for an antique mirror of some value. My client was a millionairess, and to get her the type of thing which she wanted would delight her and do my depleted bank balance quite a lot of good. I did not expect to find her a bargain; the main idea was to find the mirror which would appeal to her and which she would recognize as an investment as well as a practical thing of beauty. Within minutes of her leaving my shop a most distinguished-looking man entered and asked if I would be interested to buy a copper ship's lantern. As an after-thought he mentioned that his wife had an Italian mirror for which she paid a lot of money years ago and had now decided to sell since they had moved to a smaller house. Coincidences like this can happen but I should not have really believed this. It was the thirteenth of the month and I am notoriously superstitious. However, we arranged an appointment to see the ship's lantern and the mirror. I spent the next day visualizing the mirror—would it have cherubs on it? Surely the giltwood would be damaged—who would be available to repair it? Undoubtedly, the mirror would be 'foxed' but that would not matter. I could show it to my client in its natural state and if she wanted it re-silvered it could be easily arranged.

I armed myself with far more money than I expected to pay for it but remembering the ominous warning of 'my wife paid a lot of money for the mirror' I tucked a further 'pony' into my smaller wallet, resolving that rather than lose it I'd go the whole hog and pay even as much as the lady paid herself for it originally.

Well, the ship's lantern was produced; the type that one sees in antique shops all over the world, selling from three to five pounds anywhere. Now for the mirror. A fourteen-inch object of cold metal was thrust into my hands. To my horror I saw that it had a sort of brass frame which screamed 'Birmingham' at me.

This was one of the few moments when I was speechless. *This*, an Italian mirror—this shapeless, decrepit, badly designed, utterly *common* brass frame—an Italian mirror! Oh no! No one could play a joke like this on me. I'd been promised an antique mirror. I'd got money burning a hole in my pocket to buy and I had a wealthy client waiting and willing to give me a profit on it! How bitter can you feel? It was like the realization that there is no Santa Claus; that the streets of London are not paved with gold! This was the great disillusion to end all disillusions, a physical pain. Even a terribly bad mirror, if it had been in Italian giltwood, would have been better than this, but this. . . .! Instinct compelled me to murmur brokenly—four pounds for the two pieces—but hated the man with a great bitter hatred for making me suffer like this. My offer obviously hurt him too and I went home with my money safely tucked in my wallet and ten years stripped from my life, and a week of nightmares in store for me in which all my clients offered me 'Italian' mirrors—made in Birmingham!

There ought to be a law against it! That poor Birmingham mirror was not even old enough to have had a grandmother to have lavished love and care on it. It had always been an unhappy thing but perhaps at some date in the future another braver antique dealer than I will be called out to see a few things that 'my grandma thought a lot about' and behold! The pseudo-Italian mirror will rear its ugly head again. It ranks with the Japanese tea-service—both are quite indestructible and exist purely to annoy the poor long-suffering fraternity of antique dealers. Any grandma who 'thought a lot of' this sort of thing could only be a moron and proves the point that I frequently make, that because a thing is *old* it does not immediately become *good*. The original buyer, even a grandma, needed to have *taste*.

7

Market-day
—the Romanies' Sunday

RINGWOOD is a market town, and in common with so many of the other small towns in the New Forest area it has its days of semi-somnolence. There are some Mondays in the year when Ringwood takes on the air of being wholly asleep. There are even some Saturdays when the inhabitants of Ringwood desert their own town to jostle with the crowds in nearby Bournemouth, Southampton or Salisbury. It is on Wednesdays, winter and summer, when Ringwood can hold its own with other towns or villages, for Wednesday is market-day.

My shop has a glorious vantage point for watching the market even without moving from the house at all. For it is situated at the exact point where the cobblestones of the actual market-place first take on a faint air of sophistication and begin to call themselves the High Street. As I look from my windows it seems that this house is something of a frontier station where the old traditions of the market end and the new modern tone of the town first makes its impact. On the right of my shop the cedar-wood-fronted shops are already beginning to change the character of the town, but to the left the history of Ringwood remains inviolate. The little Market Square is dominated by the sturdy grey walls of the church of St. Peter and St. Paul. Architecturally the church is not impressive but it's beautifully sited. It stands well back from the Market Square but on a slight incline, which gives it a gentle watchful air. The sweeping grass of the churchyard with its moss-clad gravestones and the tall evergreens make it a picture-postcard setting.

Below the church, creeping right up to its very walls is the market-place. Fruit, vegetables, shrubs and plants are brought in from the surrounding countryside to be laid on the cobblestones to be sold by auction by the old-established firm of Woolley & Wallis. In the centre of the market-place there is a triangular island, marred by an unsightly lamp standard of the worst part of the Victorian era. If the original lamps were still on this standard it would be bearable. I recently found an old postcard showing the lamps and they certainly added dignity and grace to what I can now only describe as a sad eyesore in an otherwise pretty market-place. This grim reminder of the ungracious part of the Victorian age, however, is the absolute hub of the entire market, for round it revolves some of the most interesting things offered for sale. Rows of poultry-pens are erected on the south side. Facing the church side are several tables on which the smaller amounts of vegetable products are spread. Ringwood Market on any Wednesday is like some wonderful harvest festival; the fruits and flowers of the seasons are in profusion and the quality is excellent, for this area boasts many fine gardeners who are proud of their produce.

It is the small spot between the chicken-pens and the flower tables though that particularly appeals to me. For this is the 'dead stock market'. Every conceivable thing at some time of the year is offered for sale here. Oh, the wonderful joy of viewing the dead stock market early in the morning! I've had some startling purchases here. A French table can nestle in close proximity to a sack of logs, its tarnished ormolu mounts looking quite incongruous against such lowly neighbours as chicken-houses, wheels from old carts and suchlike things which, in its original state, the poor French table would never know could exist! I once bought a very fine but incredibly dirty small Georgian table from amongst the dead stock. Copper pans and bits of brass turn up regularly as well as sacks of books, shoes and clothes. There is always an element of surprise in this section of the market.

On Wednesdays I hear the first small bustles of noise coming from the market-place in the early hours of the morning and some migratory spirit arises in me. I wait for Mrs. Strong to appear in the shop, fretting if on this morning she is ever a minute late whilst on other mornings it never seems to matter. There is an urgency to leave the shop and to drift leisurely down the full length of the market stalls which spread from the actual market-place almost to the door of my shop. I pass down the double-sided row of stalls and feel at one with the stallholders. For it is here that I too once had a stall. Many years ago, when through a series of unfortunate circumstances I was down to my last pound note, I drifted unhappily into Ringwood market-place. There, laid out on the cobblestones, was a huge assortment of pots of paint. I knew a builder who would buy it so I risked fourteen shillings of my precious pound and bought the whole lot of paint. Many tins of it had a famous branded name on them and I sold them to a builder for as many pounds as I had given shillings for it. With the money I bought a frightfully worm-eaten stall from one of the Salisbury stallholders. Week after week I set up the stall with a pathetic amount of oddments on it, practically all my own possession, to be precise. I used to pray every Tuesday night that it would be fine on Wednesdays for I had only a very antique shot-ridden 'tilt' with which to cover my stall. A journey of a thousand miles begins with one step, says a Chinese proverb. The roots of my present shop are in that old market stall which I had for years. Nowadays in odd moments of pride as I sometimes pull off a spectacular deal in the shop, I am humbled by thinking of those early market days, when the present stallholders first became my friends and helped me over some difficult periods.

On Wednesdays now I can walk through the rows of stall-holders knowing that each one that I stop to talk to has indeed been a friend to me. I am still one of this strange motley fraternity of travelling dealers, and it is a good feeling. I buy fruit and vegetables from one stall, lettuce from another, flowers from another. Everyone asks kindly about the shop and they still slip an odd apple or banana in my bag 'for the boys'. They are kindly people these market traders; hard working, impervious to adverse weather conditions, selling their goods with humour and ability. Many of them are of part-Romany extraction, many are foreigners who can earn a living in no other way than this, but they have the common bond of kindness and tolerance.

During the last week when I had a stall in the market it became known that a very poor coloured trader was at last going home to Ghana. For years I had known Sammy; he had come to England to study law. Something went wrong and Sammy was unable to continue his studies, and worse still he became badly crippled. He used to set up a little card-table just across the road from me to display his tiny stock of rather inferior goods. His whole stock could not have cost more than a few pounds. Rain for Sammy was an even greater tragedy than it was for me, his legs troubled him in bad weather and it was difficult to make a living.

The stallholders would swear and curse amongst themselves, but in a rough-and-ready way everyone considered that Sammy needed looking after. One trader would bring him in from Bournemouth and so save him the agony of struggling with his suitcase and card-table on the bus. Someone would always see that he had a sandwich and a cup of tea at lunchtime. They would throw light-hearted insults at him but there was no malice in the insults. Sammy would laugh with us all. He would come every Wednesday at noon for a few minutes to my stall and tell me of his plans to return to Ghana. I promised him the best suit that my Phoenix Dress Agency could supply when he was actually certain of the date of his departure. The promise was made in the warm summer months but was not fulfilled until the first of the snow had fallen. George, the carpet dealer who had his stall next to me, said one day when we were all blue with cold:

'Our black man's going back to Ghana, we'd better do something about it.'

He borrowed a hat and took it round to all the stallholders; they gave freely although not one of us had made a day's wage on this particular day. He explained to the few customers who stood around, 'It's for Sammy, *the black man*,' and they, too, good-naturedly, added odd pieces of silver to the contents of the hat. We gave Sammy his farewell present, we clapped him on his back and insulted him as we had always done for the last four years.

I think it was the ribald insults of George that helped Sammy to carry on when he was racked with pain and home-sickness. Sickly sentiment would have done nothing, but when George screamed at him he would always slip a sandwich on the table or an odd half-crown into the saucer which poor old Sammy used as a till, and which on many days saw so little other money. He went back to Ghana; unobtrusively he slipped away from us, but I never pass his little pitch in our market without thinking of Sammy.

There are two traders who bring junk and antiques into the market on Wednesdays. I love to buy something from one whom I call 'Misery Martin'. In all the years I have known him, he has never admitted to having a good day! Trade is always *terrible* but he still comes.

The stalls trail away thinly as the street flares into the actual market-place and the weekly harvest festival takes over. The cockerels crow in their pens, the odd valuable piece of furniture droops ashamedly in the dead stock centre. The market goes on, week after week, a tradition holding its own even in these days of 'super-markets'; with their chrome, expensive fitting they cannot hold a candle to a street market like Ringwood, for they are without a soul.

If the goods displayed are a pleasure and a surprise then the people who bring the goods into the market are even more so. Every Romany in the area makes a point of coming to Ringwood Market, and the bulk of the dead stock comes from the Romany and Didicai dealers. The families from West Moors are certain to bring in all kinds of cycles 'dollied up' with harsh silver paint, the Ibsley families bring copper and brass and many families from nearby St. Leonards are certain to bring in the odd piece of furniture to add to the chaotic splendour of the 'dead stock' section. I know nearly all the Romany families in this district.

From Lyndhurst comes Ernie Veal, one of the most likable characters of the whole of the New Forest. Ernie and I are friends of long standing; we met in Lyndhurst during the war, when he rescued me from a car that had run out of petrol—miles from a garage. Since then we have done numerous deals together, from calves, cows, ducks and horses to the inanimate objects like horse brasses. Incidentally the last cow you sold, Ernie, was a barrener; you ought to be ashamed of yourself! Ernie had a rare eye for a horse; he can 'break' anything on four legs and he buys and sells with a natural *joie de vivre* which I myself try to imitate in the shop.   As I listen to the patter in the market-place I cease to be a shopkeeper. I talk with friends of old deals and of possible ones for the future, and we laugh with great good humour. Ernie tells droll stories in the easy manner of a born raconteur. Once he appeared on a Wilfred Pickles radio programme and absolutely stopped the show. When I first knew him in 1940 he was an old man. Now, twenty-one years later, he does not appear to be a day older. He has a wonderful, expressive face which a modern Rembrandt could immortalize. Ernie enters the market-place like a true prince of Egypt. Thin-featured; hook nose; sharp, alert, deep-set eyes which laugh as he tells one of his stories. He dresses carefully in the old-style manner of travellers, deep-waisted jacket with hand-stitched cuffs and revers. The traditional diklo (neckerchief) is tied around his neck and he has a fine black velour hat with a massive brim. It is a practical, warm attire for any man who spends much of his time outdoors.

'Halloo, me gel,' he yells to me across the market. 'You still in business?'

I assure him that I am indeed still in business, which really means that I am in the mood to buy whatever choice commodity he may have tucked away in his well-laden van.

'Come here then, gel,' he calls. 'See what I've got, do your old eyes good to see what I've got here.'

I move over to the van and we start an intense haggle over a bit of harness or a copper pot. It takes a great deal of backchat to settle any deal with Ernie. He puts up a fine show of spirited

61

talk and sometimes, in a particularly hard deal, he will retire inside the van giving me an expression of hurt despair.

Always money changes hands, very often readily on my part because Ernie brings salable stuff for me to see. He is too wise a bird to waste his time or mine on rubbish. We both become pleased for different reasons. On my part because I can see a decent profit in the future sale of the goods and Ernie because our deals generally take place in the early part of the morning. Ernie is a true Romany and likes to feel the touch of hard cash early in the day.

It does something to his ego. A shilling earned before the shops and the market are officially open is a source of joy to any Romany. It takes on the aspect of 'good luck money', the sign that there will be other good deals during the day.

After gossiping to Ernie I begin to drift slowly round the market looking at this and that and eternally chatting. For what good is any market-day if you can't linger with old friends to hear what is happening amongst the families in the New Forest? It is Wednesday, the day of the week for plenty of talking, for dealing, for forgetting to watch the clock. It is a day to enjoy, to sustain one until next market-day.

A light touch on my shoulder asks me to turn around to see Sonny, who wants to attract my attention. He is young and oddly good-looking. A mass of rich red hair thatches his well-shaped head and he has a mass of freckles which add to his unusual looks. With his stocky figure there is a touch of Mickey Rooney about him. Sonny is quite a lad. In the course of the time that I have done deals with him I have gathered that Sonny is a rare one for the girls. They appear to be alternately the joy and the bane of his young life. Somewhere in one of the South Coast towns, Sonny has a wife and four children tucked away in a respectable little bungalow. Yet he chooses to live in a caravan deep in the New Forest. In a moment of confidence he told me about this and I did not believe him. Later I learnt that he had spoken the truth. Sonny works three days of the week for his wife and brood, then three days for himself. This gives him enough to buy petrol, cigarettes and whisky, and from these simple amenities I suppose he feels able to face yet another week of work. Sonny is both moody and mean in character, he suffers hours of self-inflicted torture which can only be dispelled in a haze of whisky. For he genuinely loves his wife and yet is unable to find a solution to his cumbersome love life without hurting someone. Sometimes when the whisky is heavy within him he will break down and cry like a child, pouring out his sorrows. Swearing that he doesn't know which he loves best, his wife or his work, and intoning the virtues of each. But on Wednesday mornings Sonny is a clear-headed dealer more than the Don Juan of our market-place.

He deals chiefly in ex-War Department goods and he deals with a rare flair of genius. I have known him to turn over a few hundred pounds on one deal alone. I like Sonny although I can never understand his way of living. Perhaps it is his fate that he has only to flex the muscles in his brawny arms to have the local girls come running to him. He can't resist the young girls and they can't say 'no' to him. He adores his children. All are well endowed with good looks and both he and his wife take equal pride in keeping their children clean and well cared for. I know that a man is entitled to live whatever type of life that he chooses, but often I have a sneaking feeling of sorrow for Sonny. I can't help wondering why a man with so much talent for dealing should make such an unholy mess of his private life. He drives hard bargains and never hesitates to tell me that he hates any women in business. At these times we mutually despise each other. I know that if Sonny could find a man to buy the same type of things that I buy from him he would cut me dead. I would never see him again, but at the moment I am a safe nebulous figure to him. 'A dealing woman' which he loathes as much as I hate his love life. Actually I think we *enjoy* our moments of mutual hatred and it certainly keeps me on my mettle as far as buying is concerned. I don't expect any concessions and he doesn't give them, so somewhere along the line we reach a feeling of unusual understanding. But there is never the happy feeling that I get when dealing with Romanies. Sonny has a chip the size of

Cleopatra's Needle on his shoulder and sometimes he allows it to influence his work. His domestic worries colour his life. He can dream up big deals and often put them into operation, but there is always the off-chance that an altercation with some woman will upset the deal. To me, Sonny is a tragedy. The touch of big dealing genius hovers over him but it is barely skin deep. He is big-headed, obstinate and morose. Even when he is within a hair's breadth of greatness he will miss the boat. Certainly he will never be the colourful character in twenty years' time that Ernie Veal is today. Sonny has a definite intangible charm but I have never noticed any staying power in anything that he touches. Easy come, easy go, live today and be damned tomorrow is his axiom for life.

Perhaps the most unusual person who ever comes to Ringwood Market is Domenic. I love Domenic, for he has the touch of real greatness about him. He brings a romantic swashbuckling atmosphere into the market. There is an Edwardian elegance about his attire, somewhat decadent but nevertheless interesting. I like his staunch adherence to the traditions of the old-style Romany life. With it all he has an unusually intelligent brain, a thinking power that is entirely his own. He is vain and obstinate, a creature sufficient to himself. Like Ernie Veal, he was born of Romany parents and he has a pride in himself and his race that touches me greatly. He has never slept in a house and until this year has always travelled the Forest roads in the old-style, horse-drawn wagon. I have seen some exquisitely painted wagons done by his charming wife, Clarissa, a girl of quite brilliant talent and attraction. Augustus John has painted her many times and she is a worthy subject for any painter, with her long, thin face, deep-set eyes and her mass of golden hair reaching beyond her shoulders. We have all become good friends but we never encroach on each other's lives in any way. All through the winter months we do some quite stupendous deals and each one is a jewel of verbosity. Domenic works hard enough to get the right stuff to sell to me. I have known him to travel a hundred miles or so in one day. It has been worth it for he has brought back an enormous assortment of garden seats and urns as well as a collection of oil lamps. He enjoys looking for unusual things. Even if he cannot identify the object he has bought he will take a chance, just to have the fun of buying it to bring to me. Once he brought a long, low, wagon-like truck, which didn't seem practical for any purpose that we could think of. It was beautifully made. A fine slab of oak formed the top and inset around the sides were several wrought-iron rings. The wheels were very strong and sound. It was quite a little time before we worked out that the only thing that would travel properly on such a wagon (which was about seven feet long and three feet wide) was a *coffin*. Unkowingly Domenic had bought a very old bier.

I bought it from him and stood it amongst the garden urns for many months, using it for a garden table, but I was never quite happy about putting it to such a use.

One day I met a jovial fresh-faced type in the market who looked like a farmer but who turned out to be an undertaker. His pride was that he had 'three sons in the business and enough work for them all'. He came to the shop and bought the bier. It seemed an appropriate thing for him and I am sure that they would have lots of happy times together.

'Perhaps I'll find another bier for you one day,' said Domenic, when I told him that at last I had sold it. Sometimes that man carries his devotion to business too far. I feel I can bear to live without one for quite a long time.

Ringwood as a market town has so much to commend it. By its geographical position, with the lovely River Avon flowing through it, it is natural that the town is a magnet to fishermen. They come to the town with their wives who add to the brightness of the market-place with their pretty clothes and mixed accents. Ringwood people are pleasant and easy-going to welcome all visitors but they all have a fine feeling for the industry of shopkeeping. No matter how dreary other days may be, Wednesday brings a feeling of rebirth into the town. Whilst other places may boast of better architectural features, of model industries, of well-designed housing estates, Ringwood, with its age-old

Charter Market can offer a vigorous life to visitors and residents. Residents stay and visitors come back year after year.

The market is leased to the firm of Woolley & Wallis, estate agents and auctioneers, who as a firm have a long and interesting history in this area.

Presiding over the 'dead stock' market is the neat little figure of Mr. Matcham, an auctioneer who is a joy to watch and a delight to listen to as he works. His good humour and easy manners have made him a friend of every farmer for miles around.

He sells the goods easily, with all the fluency of a good auctioneer. His accent is thick with dialect and he is certainly a major asset to the market life whether he is selling chickens or dead stock. Buyers and sellers know him to be a fair man. On cold winter days he can be seen early around the market-place. Duffle-coated, well shod and always wearing the neatest of trilby hats he is as consistent as the church clock. When the wind whips across the Avon he may be practically frozen to death, but he always has the same friendly, amiable smile for everyone whom he meets.

Once, when we were talking about auctioneers in the area who had been selling some rare pieces of furniture, Mr. Matcham looked just a bit downcast.

'I only sell junk,' he said, not bitterly but rather thoughtfully.

'Ah,' I replied, 'but you sell it like a gentleman.' I meant it, too, for whatever he sells he does it with that admirable asset of charm. I like the tough, street-market auctioneers far more than I like the sleek city gentlemen who are limited to selling only rare goods. A day earning a living on a cold day in Ringwood Market would put them all in bed with pneumonia. Men like Mr. Matcham are the backbone of market-town life, as honourable and consistent as the ancient stones from where they sell the market goods.

As I look round the market-place I see many old farmers who can remember when they used to come to Ringwood Market in their young days. They had to leave home at 4 a.m. in order to reach the market in time to sell their produce, travelling from outlying districts in pony-and-traps. I look round and see the Romany and Didicai faces and marvel that this is the one day of the week when they can freely rub shoulders with the wealthier neighbours of the New Forest. This is the day when there is less likelihood of a policeman enquiring into their business. I watch the holiday crowds milling around the 'flash' stalls of the London boys who use the market only during the heyday months of July and August. There is a magical feeling of unity in Ringwood on Wednesdays. It lasts for about eight hours and then we all return to our normal way of life. The Romanies disappear into the Forest using the little-known paths. The Didicais to the encampments of Shave Green and West Moors. The holiday crowds return to their hotels and boarding houses where they wonder why they ever bought a canteen of cutlery. At home they are sure they don't need the cutlery, but under the mesmerism of a market trader people buy many things that they don't want; cheap costume jewellery takes on the attraction of real stones when displayed on a sunlit day on a market stall. It is all an illusion, but pleasant enough whilst it lasts.

The stallholders begin to pull down the tilts and pack the remains of their goods into cars and trailers. Neatly, quickly, everything ready for the next market-day in Blandford. The last of the chicken-pens are pulled down and old Irish Paddy wheels away enough empty wooden boxes to keep his fires going for many a long winter's night. As the pubs open again at 6 p.m. Ringwood is gradually getting back to normality. The Market Square is again taken over by serenely parked cars. There is a stillness where only a few hours ago there was a carefree crowd happily watching Mr. Matcham sell the chickens and dead stock. A single piece of coloured paper from one of the fruit stalls is the only thing left to remind me that another market-day has happened. Some days there is not even this memento because we have a diligent police force who studiously watch the stallholders to see that no debris is left behind. The basic pattern is the same on every Wednesday that ever comes.

I return to my shop in the High Street with reluctant steps and always on this day I think back to the time when I had my own stall in this market. I look back on the cold, dark, wintry mornings when I struggled to put up my wobbly old stall. There is security in the warmth of the shop, a sense of achievement in knowing that it is mine, but I hope I will never forget that the real roots of the shop go back to a tattered old stall on the cobblestones of the market-place. Great oaks from little acorns grow; my stall was a very little acorn indeed.

Thursday morning comes along and I am back to being just a shopkeeper again but I can't help thinking that it is one day nearer to the next market-day!

8
Too many rings

FROM the well-stocked auction rooms all over the country there comes a wealth of treasures and about 60 per cent of everything sold under the hammer finds its way into the antique and junk shops of the British Isles. Indeed, any auction room is the main artery of life for the smaller antique shop. It pays the small dealer to buy regularly at his local auction sales rooms because on the one day that you miss attending a sale that is the day when the bargain of your life slips through.

If you are in the vicinity there is a resonable chance that you recognize the bargain and ultimately you may be lucky enough to buy it. True, one man's bargain is another man's poison but it is nice to know that it is there and can possibly be yours!

Today, every London dealer treats the market-town auction room with respect, for it is here, sandwiched amongst the household furniture, rubbing noses with quite unmentionable items, that the long-looked-for, unexpected treasure can occur. True, you have to be of a patient nature, able to withstand many, many dreary 'lots' of beds, of equally dreary and terribly wearisome corny jokes, without which no auctioneer is complete. But at the end of the day you may have achieved something worth while, even if you have a decadent springless settee thrown in with the lot for good measure. For the small-shop owner the glamorous names of the world-famous London salerooms must remain a dream. They are the places where he must try to sell his bargains, not the place to buy unless on behalf of a wealthy backer.

For my part the austere and rarefied air of the Fine Art salerooms have little charm except on the occasional busman's holiday. For pure business, which can be combined with pleasure, give me the small auction rooms of a market town or the more exalted quality of a house sale, preferably in the country.

Of course there are disadvantages in buying locally. Many housewives, armed with children and knitting, take up advantageous posts in the auction rooms and with great deliberation take down with commendable solemnity the exact price of every article sold. The zeal with which this ritual is carried out always amazes me; the local housewife at a sale is far more efficient than any secretary and can always tell you the price of the most insignificant lot. All this perfection and never a stitch dropped, too! Babies are fed at regular intervals; the whole manœuvre is carried out with almost martial perfection. I frequently get lost in admiration and quite petrified by the housewife at a sale. She deserves every bargain she bids for, although in truth I don't think she goes so much to *buy* as to have a curious day out. Or perhaps the auctioneer pays a clique of housewives to come along to laugh at his jokes; after all, someone must appreciate the constant supply of hoary old chestnuts which the poor man flings out at regular intervals.

Enter Lot 234, an electric fire.

'Come, ladies and gentlemen, let me have your bids.'

Breathlessly I wait for the old, old quip to come and I am never disappointed. Here it comes. If it is a burning day in June (and such things have been known) he says:

'Plenty of cold days to come.' (Laughter in court.)

So we move on, each lot with its accompanying theme of good humour, its titter of appreciative laughter ending with a final brisk tap as the gavel meets the rostrum. Lot 234, the electric fire, is dead; long live Lot 235, possibly, with the incongruity of auction sale catalogues, a refrigerator. So it goes on and still the housewife notes each and every price with the efficiency of a super-secretary. Do not imagine either that this noting of prices finishes at the end of the sale: there is a sequel. The day following they take ghoulish pleasure in doing a *tour de force* round the antique shops, checking prices and rapidly calculating in a manner which would put any comptometer to shame the difference between purchase and retail price. The more advanced types can even work out mentally one's exact financial status, and one almost wonders if they are really a M.I.5 branch of the local Income Tax office!

Alas, it is for me to disillusion the poor hardworking house-wives who have a yen for this type of life. Underneath their very noses, before their very eyes, one of the most nefarious contraventions of the law goes on, and yet in their keenness they are un-able to see it. I refer to the workings of the technique which in the business is called 'the Ring'.

What is the Ring? Well may you ask this. It consists of a secret fraternity of dealers who gather at every view day like a crowd of vultures waiting to give the *coup de grâce* to a dying body. They come from all corners of the country, according to the degree of importance of the sale. The long and the short, the thin and the fat, the straight, slim youths and the bandy-legged old men. It is not the vagaries of their physical appearance which is frightening, it is their mentality. Many of them are aesthetic types; most of them are intelligent even if only with a one-track mind. Some have knowledge, some have not; many are just rogues battening on to a racket which is less dangerous and more profitable than robbing a bank. Although the rules of any auction room clearly state that the functioning of a Ring is completely illegal, not one auctioneer in the country, to my knowledge, has ever made any attempt to enforce this rule. The result is that local Rings function blatantly under the nose of the law and within sight and sound of the public.

How does it work, this infamy amongst the famous? It has a native simplicity, blunt and to the point. At the view day, members of this Klu Klux Klan type of brotherhood, who mas-querade under the name of honest dealers, inspect the goods offered for auction in the salerooms. The campaign for the actual selling day is arranged by a dominant character of the local dealers, a sort of accepted 'head man' or witch doctor. The campaign has all the neatness of a successful military campaign—the attack, the call-up of reserves if necessary, all is decided by these gentle warriors of our commercial age.

One man—say, a dealer from Bournemouth—will be instructed to bid on all the major pieces of furniture. Another, probably from Christchurch, will bid only on the silver, and yet another will bid on the china and porcelain, and yet a fourth, probably from Salisbury, will take on all the bric-à-brac and Victoriana. Only one member of the Ring will bid at each time and they will never bid against each other, but every aspect of the sale will be covered. This is the one certain thing which you can bet on. The sale is toothcombed on view day by the dealers of the Ring and nothing escapes, absolutely nothing. Sometimes a member of the public may throw a spanner into the works by bidding heavily against the Ring, blissfully and innocently hoping that some particular plum will fall. Now the reserves of the Ring are called up. The man bidding with the Ring will sacrifice a lot of his profit to get the thing he has set his heart on. It probably brings on duodenal ulcers quicker than anything else but the public has to be taught a lesson, and the lesson is that the dealer always wins unless he is bidding against a punch-drunk millionaire.

The only time when the Ring can be completely upset is when someone like myself decides to follow very unorthodox and completely mischievous tactics. The idea is to break into the bidding, very calmly and with complete indifference to whoever else is bidding. Break down the enemy by a game of brag, bid confidently and coldly, looking neither to right nor left and ignoring everyone else in the room but the auctioneer. Bid as if you are prepared to go on until the Day of Judgment and *sometimes* you can get a break. For the bidder on behalf of the Ring can suddenly become worried. He feels the nervous reactions of his compatriots; he is the hope of the side, the last man batting on a very, very sticky wicket and it is nerve for nerve who will give in first, the Ring or I! It becomes a terrific gamble, this attempting to pirate a piece of furniture on which the Ring has set its heart, but occasionally sheer cold nerve and the tactics of a dramatic poker-player can win.

Sometimes it is fun to leave your opponent with the piece when it has gone well over the price which you estimate they wish to pay, but I only play this game when I have had a secret 'coup' and can afford to be expansive financially. The biter can be bitten. It is a delicate part, this driving hard to the last bastion when something has to give way. Personally, at the last stroke I fall back on feminine indecision and the prize falls to my opponent. There is no sweetness in it for him; when it has gone the full range of price there will not be a profit in it for anyone. It is a dangerous game but can have its fascination, rather like walking on a tightrope over the Clifton Gorge.

I can guarantee that these tactics will always puzzle the enemy and often the veneer of many a gentlemanly (!) dealer can be cracked. At other times I can afford only to sit and watch but always with some modicum of amusement at the jiggery-pokery within the hallowed precincts of a respectable saleroom. Dear reader, the Ring operates not only in your market-town sale-rooms but in the big London auction rooms as well. It is virulent, dangerous, insidious and downright dishonest, but it works and pays mighty big dividends to the operators of it.

After the official sale the real fun begins, when the dealers gather for the thing known in the business as the 'knockout'. For now the dealers hold their *own* auction. Each man bids for the piece he personally requires and there are no holds barred either in technique or in language. It is all the same whether the piece is a bow-fronted chest of drawers worth perhaps twenty-five pounds or a Dutch still-life painting worth thousands. Suppose a chest of drawers has been bought under the official hammer for seven pounds ten shillings; in the 'knockout' it may be worth thirty pounds to one of the Bournemouth dealers. He pays this sum into the 'kitty' and the operating members of the Ring make a nice little profit of twenty-two pounds ten shillings. This, with the other money raised by a similar process of bidding on other items, is equally divided between all the members of the Ring who 'stood up' for the sale. Indeed, it is possible to make a profit simply by putting in an appearance at a sale without even wishing to buy anything for oneself. Only you, the gullible public, loses. If you once thought it strange that your late aunt's silver candlesticks didn't make the price you thought they would and fetched nowhere near the estimated insurance value, why, now you know the reason. Equally so, if you have seen a local dealer pay ten pounds for a piece of porcelain and then seen the same piece in his window for sale at fifty pounds you are bound to conclude that he is making a massive profit whilst, in fact, the poor man may be struggling to get only a most modest profit on the real cost of the porcelain. For the Ring consists of members who believe that dog eats dog and they pay well amongst themselves in this foulest of all secret societies—this Union for shrewd foxes.

For my part I blame the auctioneers for knowingly permitting this state of affairs to flourish under their gavels. In the West Country every pretence of being honest is blatantly flung to the winds. I have seen 'knockouts' taking place under the very rostrum of the auctioneer while he chats merrily to his clerk. It almost makes one wonder, does the auctioneer also get a 'cut' in the deal, or is he merely conveniently obliging or simply naive? Whatever the answer, the fact remains that the auction rooms all over England are in need of a rush of clean air, for it has been a long time since honest breaths were drawn in them.

I am told that Rings are a tradition amongst antique dealers but it is a tradition in the worst possible taste and one which the whole community could well do without. There is ample margin in the antique trade for everyone to make a good profit without misleading the public any more than is necessary. Besides, the methods of the Rings are crude and soul-destroying to everyone concerned. One thing I can state with great confidence: you have to be of really tough stamina to remain outside the Ring, for if you do every dealer in your area goes 'gunning' for you. It is only by having a complete contempt of their methods and a great deal of native cheek plus a few private 'coups' which have enabled me personally to survive. I ought to have died a thousand deaths within a few months of opening this shop in the High Street. As it is, I've been maligned, blackballed, insulted and once I was nearly beaten up. But I am of the wrong race to die easily without putting up a fight and now I can safely say I can hold my own in any saleroom in any part of England, and come away with enough stuff to call it a good day's work. This, without joining in any of the machinations of the iniquitous Ring.

I pad quietly along on a lonely trek and it has been a tough fight to make a success of being an antique dealer, but now I am firmly established and I sell my own goods to members of the 'trade' as and when I like. I've run the gambit of every form of business politics but now I am no longer sick and frightened after a day at a sale. True, the Ring have had their victories over me but I do not feel that I have given away much ground. Once, at a lovely country house sale in Lymington, I was determined to buy a magnificent French settee. Bidding desperately against the local Ring I had to pay sixty pounds for it. I got it and was delighted in the pure joy of obtaining it. When I got home I found that a member of the local Ring had taken the great trouble to guess who my potential client for it was going to be and had rung him up and divulged the price I had paid for the settee. The Ring would have liked to have bought the settee at about thirty-five pounds at the official auction and then re-auctioned it amongst themselves at about eighty-five pounds, so whoever would have bought it would have had to make a profit on eighty-five pounds plus out-of-pocket expenses for carriage, etc. True, I too had aimed to make a bit of hay whilst the sun shone and was all set to offer it to my client at a hundred pounds, so making a nice profit of forty pounds on an afternoon's work. However, on this day the Ring had really got it in for me and reluctantly I must admit that they won—on paper. I, on the other hand, now have a perfectly good Louis Quinze settee which gives me a great deal of pleasure every time I look at it. The day didn't break me either financially or in spirit. I reckon it to be as nothing to enter a saleroom and have every dealer in the area ignore me. I can even listen with tolerant amusement to hear myself discussed in rather scathing terms by men whom I wouldn't touch with a bargepole. The final insult of hearing one bright boy say loudly, 'What does she use for money these days?' has only the same effect on me as the proverbial water on a duck's back!

I walk alone and like it, and although I have one settee too many in my house at least I am free to make my own decisions, as well as my own mistakes, and if the mistakes serve to act as a lesson then they serve a good enough purpose.

Definitely there are too many Rings in existence and none of the glamour of the antique business would fade if they were exterminated. The business is big enough for every man to stand on his own feet, and if he can't do it he has the choice to get out and tackle something else or to form a limited company. In this way, assets could be united in a legalized manner which would not degrade a glorious trade whose very roots are steeped in tradition. That any beautiful work of art should be desecrated by the utter foulness of man in this way is utterly abhorrent to me. I am all for everyone making a living and being successful in business. Indeed, there is no harm in pulling off a good deal, but the members of Rings sink to the lowest degree and are compatible with receivers and fences. If you must be a rogue at least be an honest one and not a whited sepulchre!

So, if you read in your local Press that a Rembrandt has been sold for about fifty pounds at a sale in the North, please take the news with a massive grain of salt. I will always bet a mouse to a 'monkey' that the Ring was operating and the picture most certainly pulled a higher price than the fifty pounds quoted when it left the saleroom. Why some astute newshound has not yet become aware of facts like these is beyond me, but the secret workings of the Ring are as safely shrouded in mystery as is Freemasonry to the general public.

Show me any auctioneer in this country who dares to defy the Rings by enforcing only one of his own rules and I will say that he is a man of that rare calibre—a business man who has integrity.

Meanwhile we live in a system of 'I'll scratch your back if you scratch mine'. The dealer in the Ring, the auctioneer on his rostrum, the clerk at his desk. The business of antiques has reached colossal heights, the ratio of profit is possibly the highest ever known outside the gambles of the Stock Exchange. The risks are great and the men who deal purely in the glorious relics of our great historical heritage at the moment can rank only as the scum of the earth as far as business ethics are concerned.

Too many Rings, too many Rings of elderly delinquents with brains plus money. Too many Rings, too many men with bank balances at the expense of moral manhood.

That's the antique business with the lid off, the glamour and the beauty of past ages subjected to the ignoble tactics of the Ring; as degrading in principle as perverted sex, which destroys the very thing which it first sought to preserve.

Too many Rings. . . .

A system of dog eating dog and the resultant vomit which is left behind stinks to high heaven in the salerooms the length and breadth of England.

Who will have the courage to clean up the mess?

9

Loungers and browsers

BRRRRRRRH, brrr, brrrrrr goes the bell of the shop with the petulant impatience which even the smallest of bells can assume when demanding attention. Years ago I used to sit in the shop and wait for customers. That was before we obtained the full use of the premises and the living accommodation. Today everything is different. Apart from serving in the shop there is always a lot of work to be done in the back room or upstairs. Everything is peaceful enough when Mrs. Strong is on duty but it is on the days that she is on holiday or doing some shopping that the bell takes on its most insistent method of ringing. Life becomes a series of scampers up and down the stairs. I consider my ample figure ought to have fined down long ago after the amount of times I have careered down the stairs. Our bell knows exactly when I have reached the topmost storey of the house, its shrill voice reaches to the very timbers of the third storey.

Actually, I know exactly what happens. A small gremlin, who I know inhabits this place but have never actually managed to track down, takes possession of the bell when I am alone in the building. He, she or it takes a puckish delight in waiting until I have reached the top flight of stairs before it actually sets the bell in action. I know the gremlin has something to do with it because sometimes I tear downstairs to find no one in the shop. Of course, it could perhaps be the wind that blew the door open, but this has never been the house for reasonable explanations on any matter. So I have learnt to believe firmly in gremlins.

Of course, our pet gremlin can't keep up his stock of merry little pranks all the time. He has to have his off-duty moments;

probably there is a Gremlin Union or some such thing which looks after matters like this. At this time, after perhaps half a dozen useless trips to the shop to find no one there, I ignore the brrrh-ring of the bell until I hear movements downstairs, and rush down to discover a customer really is there.

'May we look around?' says a bright-faced, healthy-looking woman and her companion. It is such a question that is the opening skirmish to what can be a marathon feat of browsing.

The way in which two healthy females can go through the entire stock of an antique shop never fails to fascinate me. A horde of locusts have nothing on our browsing customers. They look, they poke, they pick things up to admire mutually. The browsers never hunt singly and they don't waste time asking many questions. There is so much to do in an antique shop. The browsers never put anything down in the same spot that it is originally found. Pairs of ornaments are ruthlessly parted from the place in the sunny window where they nestled together in dusty splendour. The unlucky objects may find themselves perching perilously on wrought-iron kettle-stands or any other dangerous place. At the end of a browsers' session the shop takes on an air of drunken disorderliness, and keeps me busy for hours. Small trays of jewellery in various degrees of value and beauty are the cause for special attention. The browsers descend on them with war-whoops of joyful anticipation. 'We adore poking round a shop like this' is the most frequent remark flung out by the female browsers. It is, of course, essentially a feminine occupation!

I don't attempt to join in the conversation unless I receive encouragement. Not because I am anti-social, simply because I am reduced to a state of complete mesmerism as I follow their darting movements. The antics of my customers are amusing. Customers? I use the word laughingly for want of a better word. For the 'may-we-look-around?' introduction rarely culminates in a sale.

Sometimes I venture to point out an item that the browsers have overlooked as I believe that the public is entitled to its full amount of fun, even if no entertainment tax is paid on visits to antique shops.

If the Government ever got round to levying a penny-a-head tax on browsers in antique shops, they would be able to take all the tax off beer and cigarettes! One day, if I ever catch up with our local M.P.s I must suggest this to them; they don't know what they are missing.

By the time that a desk in the shop has been reached the full circle of the game has been played. Up to this time, I have been prepared to watch and wait with a simple childlike patience. For I know that as long as there are shops such as mine there will always be a breed of browsers. Yet there has to be a limit, and for me that limit is reached when the first finger is placed on the desk. True, it is for sale but I also use the desk to stuff with odd bits of jewellery for repair and for an accumulation of useless information in the way of circulars.

The desk becomes a point of no return; at this time I feel duty bound to come out of my coma and to pounce. Nicely, pleasantly, but firmly.

'Have you found anything to interest you?' The innocence of the question brings the search party to an abrupt standstill. They begin to falter, uncertain how to proceed now that a third party has spoken directly to them. Faced with a direct question, the spell of poking is broken never to be regained again until, alas, the next visit. The more assured types who have served an apprenticeship in the art of browsing see the warning light. They are the ones who are able to make a dignified exit that would do justice to Sarah Bernhardt. With one hand they reach for the door handle whilst pausing to flash a sweet smile at me, and as they go they say, 'It's such a charming shop, we really will come again.' They are off as swiftly as they came.

The browsers who are only in their first year of their studies of antique-shop prowling are just as thorough as the more experienced ones. But they can never make a really fine 'exeunt left'. They fumble uncertainly with the catch of the door instead of using the handle. Worse still, they forget their parting lines and the episode has an unhappily ragged ending. Generally they get involved in a queue outside the fish-shop door.

I don't mind browsers; there is always the gambler's chance that one day they will return and, in a careless moment of rapture, will buy something. At least, the hope is stimulating to me as I clear up the disorder which they leave behind.

My real *bêtes noire* are the people who come in and ask for some rare thing, prefacing their enquiry by, 'I don't suppose you've got . . . (a Persian cat with one eye, a lamp to match the one my sister picked up in an Indian market . . . a small *oak* table with Regency legs . . .?)' The list of 'I-don't-suppose-you've-got' is infinite and never without interest.

I never express any surprise at the oddness of some of the requests that I receive from visitors to my shop. At least . . . I don't allow surprise to show. It is only when I sit down quietly at the end of the day that surprise actually sets in and sometimes stupefies me. The happiest days of my life are those when I really have got the odd thing that my customer is looking for. Consternation! The customer shows signs of being thwarted and may possibly turn dangerous. Oh disillusion! Was the odd request nothing more than a subtle new way to get into the shop to do a variation on the 'may I look round' theme?

I try very hard to make my customer feel at ease. After all, she has asked for something and I have got it. Two and two do not make four at this time in the shop. Sweet reason is flung willy-nilly to the four winds. The customer with technique rallies after the first moment of shock and sometimes we carry on a cat-and-mouse conversation. It is annoying that the article she asked for may be exactly the thing that I am showing her but there remains one last line of retreat without losing face.

The price.

The all-important question of money ruins our beautiful friendship. No customer worth her salt will ever say that an article is too much for her and there are various ways of escaping this.

The experienced ones say: 'Well, I really didn't come in to *buy* anything today. It's the end of the month.' (Or the beginning.

Even if it is, in actual fact, the very middle of the month it doesn't affect the ultimate issue at all.)

We understand each other perfectly. We smile frostily.

If I had an Oriental grandmother I would undoubtedly bow to her and she (if she had an Oriental grandmother) would return the salutation. We content ourselves with extreme politeness and bid each other 'adieu' without ill feeling. True, I often talk to myself when such a customer has left, but there is no law against that, is there?

After years of meeting people in this shop I have reached one sad conclusion. There are many women in this area who have Peculiar Husbands. Practically never a day goes by without a lady coming into the shop to look at some quite inexpensive thing. She looks, and as she looks she yearns. A small piece of jewellery or a tiny piece of brass, generally noted for its cheapness, gives her an expression that can only mean that all her life she has longed for just such a piece. She always says in a wistful manner: 'It's quite lovely. I adore it. . . .' Her voice trails away as a half-dreamy, half-frightened look comes over her face. She goes on, 'But I'll have to ask my husband about it. . . .' I am always desperately unhappy for such women. There are so many of them. I see them walking round the town very often with their better half. As they pass by I am surprised that the modern woman, with her emancipation, has not the courage to buy a five-shilling object without first consulting her husband. Surprised, too, that the old eternal Eve in any woman is no longer sufficient to wheedle her husband round to buying it for her. Naturally, it is only right when some item for the home should need to be bought after a consultation. I think this is perfectly reasonable. Yet, for any woman to have to ask her husband for something as trivial as a cheap brooch . . . I find myself becoming annoyed at the idea. I may not be able to lay claim to an Oriental grandmother, but I can positively declare that my legal paternal grandparent was an associate of Mrs. Pankhurst in her heyday. If she listens in at my shop in the High Street I know she must be turning in her grave.

My whole faith in womanhood is destroyed by such customers, but, really, it is probably an insult to the husband concerned. The twentieth-century man can't be as mean as that!

Men on their own, on the other hand, are really good customers. They are decisive in asking for what they want. A few enjoy a little haggle about price. I admire them for this. After all, everyone loves a bargain. I have one male customer who comes to the shop only once a year. A few weeks before Christmas he arrives, armed with a long neat list. It contains the names of the people for whom he wants to buy presents, and these include the name of a ninety-seven-year-old uncle. Years ago, this uncle was a problem to both of us. I learnt that he had everything. The things that one can give to a wealthy nonagenarian are, of necessity, limited, but we could not bear to be defeated. Between us, throughout the years, we have always found something for the old uncle. I have never met 'Uncle' but I feel as if I know him quite well. When my client comes each year he tells me details of the old gentleman's state of health and what he thought of last year's present. The most successful thing we ever gave him was a cut-glass carafe with a matching tumbler. I use the word 'we' because I always feel as if the present is from both my client and myself. I often think of the old dear enjoying his nightcap of whisky-and-water from my cut-glass carafe.

As Christmas approaches I find myself wondering if Uncle's name will be on the list again. Indeed, I dread the time which must inevitably come . . . it will be a day of personal sadness.

I get the 'loungers' in my shop as well as the browsers. They enter languidly as if they are sure it is all going to be a desperate waste of time. A frightful bore, but it is against some inherent principle in their make-up to pass a shop such as mine. Generally the loungers are too tired to say 'good morning'. They mooch into the shop, casting a tired eye around for the nearest thing to lean on. That the item chosen as a leaning-post may be quite unstable doesn't enter into the matter. Life is obviously so completely insupportable and so they must lean on something, if only to give them the strength to yawn.

I don't waste much time on these types at all. They bring out the worst in me and particularly as I am getting older. Besides, yawning is catching and I never want to be caught in the vortex of being bored with living. Not only do the loungers lean on slender *torchères* but they expect me to parade my goods in front of them.

The subtle approach in sales technique is lost on loungers; one has to be quite blunt. I find that bustling around in my busiest mood, with the feather duster aimed at the thing they are leaning on, works wonders. I wield that feather duster as if it were a blunt instrument. Loungers loathe it. . . . they get a sense of insecurity, and they go.

At last—a victory for me.

Even the weather can bring its trials and tribulations right into the shop. A shower of rain can fill up the place until it looks like a football match. A flash of brilliant sunshine brings people in to get a breath of air from the electric fan. The fugitives from the vagaries of our English climate are not a bad lot, though. I can even sympathize with holiday-makers who have young children who have exhausted themselves by eating iced lollies.

Perhaps the most tiring customers are the ones who start an intelligent conversation, guaranteed to delude the poor shop-keeper into thinking that they are serious buyers. These are the insidious ones. Just when I think I am bringing off a prospective sale my customer makes frantic signs to someone in the street, or maybe over my shoulder towards the fish shop.

'Oh . . . there's Auntie . . . she's got the fish now . . . I must fly. . . .' Away she goes, leaving me standing in dumb indignation holding a plate in my hand. This type of customer never knows how near she is to being attacked with a not blunt, but equally effective, object whizzing close to her head. I thoroughly object to having my shop used as a waiting-room cum annexe to the fish shop.

It's all in the day's work, though, and towards most of the people who visit my shop I have quite an affection. Browsers, loungers, down-trodden women frightened of their husbands.

They are all part of the occupational hazard of having a well-situated shop in the High Street. It takes all kinds of people to make an antique shop.

Every Christmas I raise my glass and drink a toast.

'To the customers. . . . Bless them all.'

Not forgetting the Gremlin, of course.

Tan his hide off!

ONE day four Didicais came into my shop to try to sell me a ring. They were an oddly assorted crowd: two young men, a middle-aged woman of ample proportions and a pretty young girl. The older woman took a nice five-stone opal ring in a Victorian setting off her finger. I noticed that the ring was heavily grimed at the back as if she had worn it to work in the fields. I know that many Didicais wear even their best rings to work in the fields, even though such work is often of a dirty nature such as pulling sugar-beet. So it was no surprise to see a very lovely ring in such poor condition with much of its charm and lustre hidden by dirt. Looking back on the matter, I should have realized that it was unusual for a Didicai to wear an opal. They favour plain gold or silver rings but of course there are always exceptions to every rule. They started to tell me a hard-luck story of how they had hit a bad spell and needed money; and threw in a little colour to the story by implying that they blamed the bad-luck properties of the opal for this spell of ill luck. It sounded reasonable enough at the time and I bought the ring for a few pounds. I knew the youngest of the boys as being a member of a poor local family of Didicais but I could not place the older man or the women. I dismissed the matter by thinking that they were possibly relations passing through from Somerset who had teamed up with Hampshire relations during a lean period.

I cleaned the ring and then forgot about it. Within twenty-four hours I received a visit from the local C.I.D. who came to the shop. To my horror he enquired about the opal ring which I had put in the window. He explained that someone had broken into a house and that amongst the jewellery missing was an opal ring. The detective questioned me thoroughly to see if I had bought anything else from the Didicais. I was thankful that I could say with truth that the ring was the only item offered to me. I began to think there was something in the superstition that opals are unlucky. I could feel that it was certainly going to be an unlucky day for me. The dismal prospect of being tabbed for evermore as a receiver in stolen property appalled me, and I hastened to assure the detective that I had no reason at all to suppose that the story the Didicais had told me was anything but true. To my relief he seemed satisfied, but warned me that I should have to appear in the local court to give evidence and to identify the ring. The thought of having to waste a day in court annoyed me as much as having been caught by a Didicai into buying stolen property. The detective took the ring. By the end of the day I was convinced that I, too, would end up in the dock. It's a dreadful thing to have a fertile imagination. This was one of the days when it did me no good at all.

Next day I could think of nothing else but the affair of the opal ring but by this time I was more upset by the fact that I knew the parents and relations of the younger of the boys. I knew them to be decent hardworking types of the poorer Romany forest families and I knew that they would be very upset about their son.

In due course I was told to appear at the magistrates' court at 10.30 on a Thursday morning. I arrived in good time and waited in the foyer of the courtroom. Within a few minutes the detective who had come to the shop arrived with two ladies. One was elderly and very well dressed, and in the course of the next half-hour I learnt that she was the owner of the ring and that her younger companion was her friend who had come to give her moral support. They were both well educated but not as depressed as I was. Then the family of the young local boy arrived. The father, a huge good-looking man, stalked into the courtroom without saying a word to his wife. She was a prematurely aged-looking Romany, good-looking in a florid way but not of the cleanest type. The room was small and the normal smell of humanity was soon apparent. I had not seen the woman for some time and was surprised to see the change in her. Her body was completely bent with rheumatism and to walk even a few steps obviously caused her pain. Her hand gripped a rough ash stick. She was so obviously in a distressed state that it would have been a hard heart that could not forget the smell of unwashed humanity in order to talk to her.

It was pathetic to see how pleased she was to see someone whom she knew.

'Fifty years usn'm been in the Forest,' she said, the words alternating with robust sniffs. 'Never been in a place like this'n afore.'

At this remark the two women who were the victims of the robbery looked up. They must have seen that the old gypsy woman was genuinely distressed and, although her grief was made repulsive by the wet sniffs, there was no doubt that she was sincere. The owner of the ring began to talk to her companion in the clear, well-modulated voice of the educated. 'Those dreadful gypsies who live in the Forest. It's time something was done about them. . . .'

The companion responded with a clucking noise of sympathy that served to encourage a further tirade against all gypsies and the young boy's family in particular.

Between the insidious flow of genteel abuse, the clucking companion and the sniffing moans of the gypsy woman, I began to feel thoroughly uncomfortable. Feeling mean, I tried to move along the wooden bench, not so much to escape from the gypsy as to gain a few moments in order to marshal my own thoughts. The gypsy's eyes followed me, like the brown, frightened eyes of a forest animal, and in that moment I felt a surge of intense sympathy for her. There was sheer animal terror in her face. Impulsively, I deliberately went to sit by her side.

She was so eager to talk, pathetically anxious to tell someone of the virtues of her son to counteract the list of vices which the victim of the theft was now recounting with monotonous regularity.

'Got into bad company he has, missus,' the gypsy said. 'That other told him 'twas easy to get extra money. You knows yerself the young 'uns like a bit of extra money.'

I began to see it all so clearly. There was something of the slick spivvy type about the older man and some of the old forest boys are easy victims to brave talk.

'Mind you,' said the old woman, 'when hissen favver knew, he took his belt to the boy and he fair tanned his hide off young 'un.'

I could imagine the father doing this. Remembering the large, thick, typical Romany belt which he wore, with the shining brass buckle, I felt sick at the thought. I knew the father to be a fine enough man. He would be sentimental with his children, but he had something of the patriarchal instinct in him. Whatever punishment the court might deal out to the boy, I bet he would not forget any tanning he had from his own father. I wondered if anyone on the Bench would know this, but doubted it. Although the average gypsy is indulgent to very young children to a point of spoiling them, when they become men they must take any punishment that comes. The father would tan his son with a ferocity that is hard for a Gorgio to understand.

I was the last person to go into the court after sitting for two hours with the victim and the accused one's mother. It was almost a relief to go into the courtroom. It had been a nerve-racking experience, this battle against my ears. On one side, well-bred voices breathing righteous indignation against gypsies, and on the other side the old gypsy, her grief turned to sobs and moans and finally a dramatic calling upon God to witness that never before had her family suffered as much as she was suffering. I wanted to scream to everyone to stop.

As I went into the courtroom I saw that it was full of Romanies. Practically every member of the young boy's family was there and every other family in the area had sent a representative. They sat so still and quiet that the dark lively faces which I remembered seemed like strangers to me. As I looked at the magistrate—a woman—I thought that her face seemed more kindly and sympathetic than the Romanies, who were sitting like an enormous jury to see one of their own kinsmen tried.

The accused men sat miserably, each with his own solicitor. The spiv-type looked sullen but reasonably calm. The boy was crying bitterly. He had a tough little face and every other time I had seen him he had played at being a man. Today he was a child —old before his time—and he looked as if he was still remembering the effect of his father's belt tanning his thin, stringy body. The father had done his duty by hiring a very good solicitor for the boy—a typical Romany touch.

I could imagine his saying, 'I got a good 'un to speak for the boy.' And he would slap his pocket to indicate that he could pay for a solicitor.

I fought against any feeling for the young boy. After all, he was accused of a crime, an offence against society, but he looked so raw and defenceless as he sat, quite unable to control his tears.

My evidence took very little time and soon I was back in the foyer. The old gypsy was sitting miserably in the corner of the oak settle, her face bloated with unshed tears.

'How was it, missus?' she asked.

'It will go to the Quarter Sessions,' I said. 'I expect your boy will get probation when he comes up at Winchester.'

'Oh,' she said quite blankly, not understanding a word I was saying.

Suddenly, I felt bitter that no one had taken the trouble to explain to her just what was likely to happen to her son. I knew little enough myself about court proceedings and wondered if there was such a thing as a court missionary who could help her. I afterwards learnt that there was no such thing at a local magistrates' court like this one. Again, as I often felt when talking to gypsies, I wished that there was a modern George Borrow to appear in the New Forest. There is so much that we take for granted which our New Forest gypsies do not understand, particularly the older ones such as this woman represented. If someone could have talked to her, taking the patience to explain in simple language what was likely to happen, it would have been a good thing. The woman was sick with the worry of the moment and with fear at her surroundings and she was physically ill as well. I talked to her as well as I knew how, fretting at my own inadequacy at such a moment and finally being reduced to mere words of personal concern for her.

As the rest of the people streamed out of the court, a woman was saying that it had not been such a strain after all. Really she had found it most 'entertaining' and that a relation of hers who wrote scripts for the B.B.C. would have been fascinated. Good for him, I thought, if he can be fascinated by the sight of human misery.

The local detective took the owner of the ring and her companion home in a police car. The father of the boy appeared. He greeted me briefly, his face firm and set like a carved image. 'Come on, missus,' he said to his wife. I noticed that he helped her down the few steps from the foyer. I watched them walking up the street. The large Romany man in silent dignity and the bent old woman hobbling painfully at his side.

Because I am young enough to walk quickly I soon caught them up. I knew that they lived in a remote part of the Forest some miles away.

'How are you getting home?' I asked.

'We'm walking up to Poulner,' said the man.

I was horrified. Poulner is a pleasant enough walk on a fine day, but for this old woman it would be agony.

'Isn't there someone to give you a lift?'

'Old woman and me, we'm walk to Poulner. Our Nelson 'ul meet us there with pony.'

It was useless for me to offer to help them. This was not a time to suggest that I drove them to Poulner. The man would refuse. They wanted neither Romany nor Gorgio with them at this moment. I walked with them in silence to the edge of the town where the by-pass escapes the shops, and watched them on their way.

Two more gypsies walking along the road to Poulner would mean nothing to any passer-by.

I went back to the shop, miserable and unhappy.

Somewhere in our well-regulated system of society there are such moments as this. When a tiny sense of shame creeps in, that in my own secure life there is the knowledge that there are people in the Forest who need a helping hand. Broken down, it had simply been a day spent in a police court. A crime had been committed and would be expunged by the normal resources of the law.

The boy would never know the misery and fear he had caused his mother but . . . he would remember the day his father tanned his hide off. Probably he would remember this long after his period of probation was over.

As for me . . . I never see an opal ring without seeing the big brass buckle of a leather belt. . . .

I think I learnt a lot in the foyer of that courtroom.

II

Any early porcelain
or Georgian silver?

ALWAYS in the early hours of Monday morning they come—a vast horde of well-dressed, efficient men, popping in and out of antique shops from Bournemouth along the coast to London. This is their life, moving from one shop to another, seeking for the treasures which may crop up in the small shops. The Portobello Road merchants are 'regulars' and have a gayness of heart which is characteristic of the born dealers. They want the good stuff like anyone else but they buy the ordinary things as well, anything that they can see a shilling profit in when they show it on their stall or in their own shop. These are the boys I like, the man who will drift in on a wet Monday morning and make a pile of things on the floor of the shop and say, 'Now, make me a good price for the lot.' This way of dealing I can understand. The affair is happy, I put a realistic price on the things; there is a little backchat but the main thing is that if the Portobello boy stays an hour he *buys*. He doesn't waste time telling you when he last bought a Monet in a small shop for five shillings and sold it for a monkey. He gives his mind to the thing of the moment, and that is weeding out from your establishment the items which he can sell in London. He is a man used to making on-the-spot decisions; he rarely has a partner whose views he has to ascertain before he pays out anything over a fiver. I've had some fine deals with my Portobello Road boys, and they must be happy too, because they come back, week after week, and it is a real pleasure to do business with them. Oh yes, there are the 'wide boys' too,

93

but these I understand also and we have a mutual respect for each other.

On the other hand we get the other sort of dealer. Elegant men who, when the facts are broken down, are really only *employees* of the big London galleries and fine-art establishments. These are the dangerous ones. The smooth line of talk, with eyes darting all round the shop hoping to find the little something that you, as a poor, ignorant, peasant type of shopkeeper do not realize is of value. Inevitably the first question after the courteous 'Good morning' is 'Have you any early porcelain?' or, alternatively, 'Have you any Georgian silver?'

They follow this up with, 'I am always in the market for anything before 1800.' My goodness, who isn't, in this antique game?

Seriously, I wonder how many people buy Georgian silver only to sit on it waiting for a passer-by to call to buy it! I've often bought 300 oz. of silver in one week but by Saturday I've 'phoned someone and sold the lot. It isn't the fine stuff that is hard to sell, the only difficulty is finding it in the first place. Now, when I have anything good, I divide it amongst my regular 'boys', and I look after the ones who buy the rough bits of copper and brass, week after week. These men are the bloodstream of my bank balance. Not the seeker of the one rare piece once a month, I can sell *that* without effort. The 'any early porcelain' type is my particular *bête noir* in the trade. The stuff he is looking for can generally be found only in museums; everything you show to him would be 'knocked' (i.e. derided). 'Too plain', 'too late', 'not expensive enough', 'too dear', the phrases rip out with monotonous regularity.

Once I had the biggest pile of Georgian silver which I've ever bought stuck in my back room. I bought so much that it nearly broke me; I don't think I had two pound notes to rub together on the morning after I bought it. I badly needed to sell that silver and at a decent price. Two representatives of a well-known London firm came into the shop and began to sniff around. The younger one murmured to his companion: 'I don't suppose we'll find anything here to interest us! Not our class of stuff by any means.' I was obviously meant to hear this remark and be duly humbled, a young beginner showing off his cleverness in being able to recognize a country cousin! His chances of buying anything from me were rapidly eliminated, and when he said, 'Don't you *ever* get anything nice in this place?' he started on what had to be a very long, long period of for ever goodbye. I thought of the load of Georgian silver in my little back room; I looked at the bland boyish face on the little London toff and very pointedly I held the door open. They went!

Perhaps you will think that one man's money is as good as the next. Not in the antique business. I can sell something to one of the slick London operators, and that is the last I'll see of him for a year. He's had his little plum and I become as forgotten as last year's autumn leaves. Mingle my good stuff with other things for the Portobello boys and I take out an insurance that I'll sell them something for the next fifty-one weeks left in the year.

Also, if I am short of anything myself I can tip them off and the chances are that within a week they will bring it to me. They make a profit, I satisfy my client and so we are all happy. The 'any Georgian silver' type of enquirer doesn't give a damn for anything except the off-chance of being able to pull a fast one on you at some time or another.

The only thing I've learnt from the fine London types is to recognize a bit of good tailoring when I see it. For they dress very nattily and correctly, complete to the old school or regimental tie. They wear cravats with tiepins and single, very-well-cut intaglio rings or seals. They even wear gloves, and are indeed the modern dandies of the antique world. I like this; a well-dressed man is a pleasant person, but not to do business with. Art and beauty are far more commercialized by this type of buyer than by anyone else. He is a highly trained representative of a *firm*; he seeks treasures for his lords and masters and there is rarely any tenderness in his approach to a fine piece of porcelain. In all its beauty of colour it is reduced to so much L.S.D. with the accent on commission. They have knowledge and ability but someone forgot to put a heart in the working model.

I'll back my rumbustious Portobello boys any day against the elegant operators who work for someone else. 'Any old iron' has a far more honest ring in my ears than the mincing tones of 'Have you any fine porcelain or Georgian silver?'

12
The desk

IT WAS one of those rare, swelteringly hot days in an English summer when I decided with great solemnity that I was part of the world of Big Business. The knowledge dawned on me slowly but when it did I felt the vital importance of it. So I went to the store-room and picked the most magnificent desk which I could find. I decided now to have an office, a mysterious 'inner sanctum' where deals of great importance could be done with the aura of sane austerity which is part of the world of Big Business. No more laughter on the stairs; no more lusty jokes in the room at the back of the shop; all this must be changed. I vowed that the next time I heard any of the staff remark, 'The Old Girl's in rare form today', I'd reprimand them primly. I toyed with the idea of the staff calling me 'Madame' but the only madames I know are in France and *they* owned 'not quite nice' little establishments (but very profitable) through which one enters via a bead curtain and often has to leave by a most weird back-door route. No, I eliminated the 'call me Madame' motive. Time would provide the solution.

Well, I got the desk and after much lugging and tugging we got it upstairs into a small room on the door of which I printed a large notice in good old English script—OFFICE. The desk was very large and looked very bare, not at all like the desks in offices of my friends. So I placed on it massive silver inkpots and a leather blotter which I bought in a rash moment in Venice and never dared to use, for it looked so pretty. However, there must be a first time. I dragged long-forgotten pen-stands from the nether regions of the shop, a quill pen and a collection of gold and silver

97

pencils, a large silver cigarette-box which cost me a fortune to fill up. No more rummaging for a crumpled packet from the mysterious regions of my handbag; I'd thrust the silver box under their noses and that would be that. Even after all this effort there seemed to be something not quite right, so I remembered that all the best offices had a well-arranged bowl of flowers at one end of the desk generally placed with love and care by a secretary. I knew if I waited for my staff to do this I'd wait a long time, so I hied myself to the florists and bought myself a wonderful bunch; grabbed an impressive bowl from the shop, and up the stairs to do my own inspiration of a floral display. I regret to say that my staff were gathered for their 'elevenses' at this moment and I distinctly heard someone say, 'Coo, she's in a rare old barmy mood today.' In my new-found austerity I decided to ignore it, and hastened to this business of suitably arranging a bowl of flowers. I had in my mind's eye a little something that I had seen at a flower show in the summer, where the flowers all lean with great elegance to one side whilst a triumphant arch of colour twirls and twists to the other side. It's the sort of thing every member of the Women's Institute can do with the greatest aplomb whilst nursing the baby with one hand and treadling a sewing-machine with their feet. Dead easy! I got the twisted tortured look all right but I couldn't manage the vague, ethereal suspended-in-air technique of the centre branches. The result was terribly reminiscent of a thing I saw in a modern art show (The Unknown Political Prisoner) by a man called Reg Butler. Great gobbets of wire spewed up from the water (I know I should have bought Flora-pac) and the flower heads had a faded 'Maud-has-been-into-our-Garden' look. With a sigh I grabbed the lot, closed my eyes, put the crumpled chicken-wire (so well recommended by all our best women's magazines) into the waste-paper basket and started again. This time I picked a tall glass vase with a wide, jamjar-like neck and stuck the lot in, just like that. Plonk! They didn't look any *worse*! Whilst there was not quite a professional look and no one's secretary would ever put flowers on a desk like that, well, the colours were nice and the flowers suddenly seemed to have quite pretty faces, so the general effect was pleasing, if only to me. I have to face it, not even Constance Spry herself could have given me that *je-ne-sais-quoi* touch which all my female friends seem to be born with, that touch of genius with arranging flowers.

Ah well, back to the desk. Even with the blotter, pens, pencils, inkstand and flowers there was still plenty of space, so I put the children's photographs one on each side, in silver frames of course. They didn't show up very well and I realized I had no lamp. Down to the shop again; put the best lamp on the desk (to hell with the expense, this is an antique dealer's office, not the Labour Exchange). Ah yes, an 'in-and-out' tray and the telephone. Now things were beginning to take shape. I hadn't had any letters that morning, so I clamped a pile of typed book catalogues in one tray. It all looked most magnificent.

One more thing, a series of paper-knives; had to have those; so I arranged a fearful display of these in strategic points round the desk. I would lean back in my chair and toy with a paper-knife; all the best people do this, even estate agents. Chair? Can't have a desk without a chair; quick rally, trying a few chairs for size and comfort. Yet another chair; this time for potential clients. Not too comfortable this time, we don't want them here for the day. By now the whole office had taken shape, and really nice it looked. Only one thing worried me. There wasn't an inch of space any-where to work. If I ever did any clerical work at this desk it would be a miracle!

Well, this was really only a set piece for a delightful act. If I wanted to type I could still use the kitchen table.

I told Mrs. Strong, my most valiant right hand and manager-ess of the shop (five feet nothing of moral strength), that if anyone came to see me she must show them into my 'office'. Normally she is very quick on the uptake, but at times I think she delights in being aggravating. This was one of the times. I had to explain in the greatest detail and show her personally which room I had now decided was an office and indeed point out the notice, spelling out the O.F.F.I.C.E. very quietly to her. She inspected the desk with the most expressive of silences then said in the sour voice she generally uses when she gives me her notice (the third Friday in the month voice):

'You've forgotten the ashtrays—a fine mess I'll have to clean up if you don't supply ashtrays.'

I felt this was just the tiniest bit unjust, as I don't smoke myself and all my friends are great adepts at delicately aiming ash into vases and suchlike receptacles. Still, I remedied the omission and looked appealingly at Mrs. Strong.

'All right?' I queried.

'Hmn,' she sniffed. 'All right for *some*.' And with this some-what ambiguous statement she trotted off and went into a mad frenzy of cleaning copper with much noise and attack, a sure sign that she is really cross with me. Mentally and darkly I reminded myself that I would get into a really businesslike mood one day; after all, I *am* bigger than she is! But it would never work; she has me nicely tamed to eat out of her hand.

Well, all through the morning I saw clients in my office. Five people brought things in to sell me. One knocked over the flowers; another brought a child who dived for the quill pen and screamed blue murder when I tried to extricate it by force, so it got broken in the struggle. Children of the Welfare State are frightfully strong today and win all battles! The third person nicked two of the silver pencils when I left the office to go down to the shop. The fourth picked up the picture of my youngest son and said: 'Oh, is that the *thin* little one? He's the same age as my Peter but of course only half the size.' Obviously implying that I starve my poor little lad. The fifth caller was my old friend Cecil, artist and business man with a nasty sense of humour which generally brings out the worst in me. He looked around the room, took the 'office' notice from the door, put it in the waste-paper basket, sat in *my* chair instead of the visitors' one; flipped his cigar ash into the waste-paper basket and promptly set it on fire. We beat it out with the now sad-looking flowers, plus pouring on the remains of the water until only a thick, acrid, cough-making fug of smoke remained.

As the mistiness clears I am aware that Cecil is taking a more-than-mannerly interest in my desk, pulling out drawers, looking for woodworm in the corners, for all the world behaving like a dealer before he puts in a bid for a piece of furniture.

'How much?' he says, in that crude, blunt, down-to-earth manner so typical of dealers.

Indignantly I splutter, 'It's—it's not for sale.'

By now he is squirming his six foot two inches of thinness into convulsions which appear to be caused by a paroxysm of laughter at my reply.

I decide to be firm. 'Don't you think you can come into my office making bids for furniture—you—you arson fiend!'

(Where, oh where, is that simple calm air, the peacefulness of other offices? . . .)

'Never known you not to be open for a bid on anything,' he says. 'Are you feeling well?'

'Of course I'm well,' I yell. 'But I want a comfortable little office all neat and nice where I can see my clients, with a desk in it, and this desk happens to suit me.'

'Aha,' he says, 'one of *those* days.' He gave what he meant to be understanding, uncle-like 'clucks'. 'Be reasonable, my darling girl; I've got a client who wants a Victorian kneehole desk. Give me a price and let's get down to business.'

Already the brisk lines of sales talk are sparking up in my mind and the thought of a real office already takes on the vagueness of a dream.

'We-ell,' I say in my best no-nonsense voice, 'you know how hard it is to find desks like this. . . .'

But I'm losing ground all the way for we know each other too well. So I sit on the clients' chair and watch him flip fivers from his wallet.

'I'll tell you when you stop,' say I kindly.

'To hell with you!' he says. 'I'll give you fifteen pounds and not a penny more.'

'Fifteen pounds for this! Save your breath, it's not worth taking it downstairs. I paid more than that for it.' (Which in truth I did.)

You can see that it is now becoming painful to him but he does a quick recap and flips another fiver on the top of the other three. 'Twenty pounds, and that's the lot.'

By now he doesn't seem at all like a friend!

But I am getting into my stride. I've almost forgotten about the office lark and I suddenly realize for whom my good friend Cecil wants the desk. After all, it has been a bad morning on the whole and I may as well make the best of it and recuperate the cost of the flowers.

'Twenty-five, and I'll say nothing about the waste-paper basket you have ruined.'

This really strains our friendship to its utmost limits. I can feel it hurting him a lot and almost I suffer with him. We sit in stony silence for a few moments, eyeing each other like sparring partners.

'Twenty-two pounds ten, but I'll give you those ear-rings you like so much.' He flings the words out almost maliciously.

Really he is cheating, for I'd get the ear-rings from him in any case, but twenty-two pounds ten is a fairish price so I decide to be magnanimous.

'Well, as it's for you, it's a deal.'

Good humour is restored; he has the desk for his client; I have the cash. We laugh as we both sweep the now ridiculous clutter from the surface on to the floor, on to the chairs, anywhere. Down the stairs we lurch with the desk, out to the waiting van. We almost catapult Mrs. Strong into space as we go past; miraculously she is quite pleased with everything, chiefly because she has a soft spot for Cecil, I think. For me, however, she manages a parting shot.

'I *knew* that idea wouldn't last for long. An office in *this* place. Pah!'

The wretched woman's always right. If I don't sack her soon I'll get a terrible inferiority complex!

We all end up sitting on the stairs drinking coffee and it's 'business as usual' at the Shop in the High Street.

13
Cool cats
and an old square

ON SATURDAY mornings our shop is invaded by a steady stream of the youngsters of the town, and often a good sprinkling of students from Bournemouth. The herd instinct is heavy amongst many of the present-day young people. They flow into the shop in batches of six or more and present a problem for Mrs. Strong and myself. For, alas, some of the sweet young things have a very light-fingered touch, particularly when handling jewellery. They seem to have a peculiar desire to obtain a thing whether they have money to buy it or not, and many times we are reduced to gently but firmly asking if a ring on a finger has been 'forgotten'. Sometimes tact and temper is strained to breaking point when we say, 'Oh, you did decide to buy the little charm after all, I see you have it in your bag?' Sometimes we have had to call in the police and then there follow weeks of waiting for a quite trivial case of petty thieving to be brought to the magistrates' court. There are often tears, pleas and promises and, worst of all, there is the waste of time for a number of people. Often if a youngster steals anything it is not of very great value, but it is the antique dealer who pays in the long run. A day at the police court can often mean the loss of some important business.

I like young people, but I find it increasingly difficult to understand some of the types who come to the shop. We get the slim young girls with dainty twenty-one-inch waists which they insist on disguising by wearing awful heavy fishermen's knitted sloppy-Joe style of woollens. They saunter into the shop with drooping shoulders, which no amount of physical-culture classes at school can succeed in straightening. They are languid, blasé and wise beyond their age. Some quite pretty girls come here about once a month wearing black nylons, winkle-picker shoes with pencil-slim, straight black skirts or tight cat-pants, and they look *awful*. Their hair hangs in long lank masses over their shoulders or perhaps is scraped back into a tight pony-tail.

The cool young girls seem to do so little with the normal attributes of youth, which makes me feel something like sorrow for them. A pretty girl, neatly dressed, is a pleasant sight. In so many girls today, the sweet fresh sparkle which I always associate with youth is missing. We see more drooping mouths today than rosebud lips, and crayon distorts the eyes to form demonish contours which nature would scorn to produce if left to herself.

As I stand in the arched doorway leading from the shop to the house I see them all, I am conscious that between these girls of perhaps twenty years and myself at forty there is more than a life-time dividing us. I want to understand them, I want to find some affinity with them and I am conscious of failing to do so. So many of the young people today do not seem to have a period of adolescence, there is no subtle blossoming from childhood. One day they are mere children and the next day they are adults. It is too sudden for an old 'square' like me to comprehend.

The young men who come into the shop are slim, but often as sloppy in their movements as their female companions. In dress there is little to distinguish one sex from the other. They have long hair, often artificially curled, and their eyes have the dead look of people who have crammed the experiences of a normal lifetime into too short a period.

'Have you any knives or daggers?' the boys ask, for the youth of today has a macabre taste when they enter an antique shop and I am conscious of the terrifying underlying desire for destruction which lurks behind the youthful eyes. Too many knives are sold from antique shops to decorate the rooms of some student and then revert back to their original purpose, that of destruction. I never read a newspaper reporting a murder where the weapon used has been a dagger without feeling a shiver run up and down my spine. The knife or dagger could have come from such a shop as mine.

'Have you any knives or daggers?' asks a young boy again, and if I shake my head, they shrug their shoulders and again we lose the power to understand each other. At once we are in different worlds and for once the shop cannot bring us for one moment a feeling of unity.

Mostly the young people who come to the shop are quite harmless, but sometimes they can have the power to cause a feeling of unrest in me. Last year, on a warm night in June, I was working in the shop when the High Street was rocked with the noise of several motor-bikes tearing through the town doing a round-the-houses rodeo. It was the beginning of a new era for this market town. The 'ton' boys had arrived. The motor-cyclists did a round of the town and then came to rest outside my shop. The black-clad figures dismounted and looked in the window. Seeing me in the shop they tried the door, but I indicated that I was closed. They hammered noisily on the door making the glass tremble with the unaccustomed violence. It seemed possible that an awkward situation could arise. I suggested pleasantly enough that they should go away but they took no notice. The only thing to do was to 'phone the police.

'Have they actually hurt you, madam?' asked the voice of the policeman at the end of the 'phone. I had to admit that nothing had happened beyond the annoyance of having the shop door nearly knocked down plus a fair amount of unusually bad language. I returned to the shop to find that the letter-box had been pushed open to its utmost width and that a mass of dirty fish-and-chip papers had been pushed through. The youths were still leaning against the walls of the porch. I continued to work but it was a very uncomfortable evening until they went away.

The same thing happened for five or six more nights until my nerves were becoming quite frayed. 'Phoning the police did not seem to bring any relief; they were obviously not concerned unless I could guarantee that a corpse would be found in my shop.

On the other hand I did not see why I had to try to do my normal work in the shop whilst suffering from a flow of bad language. I also hated picking up the beastly fish-and-chip papers.

On an impulse I opened the door.

'Don't you think you could move along?' I asked, very patiently.

They eyed me over insolently.

'Who's going to make us?' said one of them. The remark brought forth roars of laughter from his companions.

'I am,' I said, very quietly. They looked puzzled, then as I moved back into the shop they followed me in. I knew I was playing a dangerous hunch but it had to be done. Apparently the law is quite willing for them to stand in the porch or lean on my window, but once they were in my shop making filthy remarks, it would become a different thing.

'I think you had better leave this shop,' I said.

They began to pick things up in the shop, taking no notice of me except to swear, obviously thinking it would annoy me as much as anything.

I picked up a whip which I had put near the door from the house to the shop. Desperate illnesses need desperate remedies.

'If you don't go, quietly, I'll use this.'

They stopped prowling around the shop, looking uncertainly at me and then at each other. I was scared to death and could only pray that my nerves would outwit their loutish manners. I am sure that they meant only to annoy me, but after five nights of insults and bad language I was completely fed up. I raised the whip. 'Get out!' My voice was harsher than I have ever known it to be.

They shambled towards the door; the last boy spat on the floor as he passed me. The action really made me see red. I raised the whip and flicked the hand of the youth who had spat. He yelled like a scalded cat, and to my complete astonishment they were gone, moving like greased lightning towards their motor-bikes. I continued to flick the whip towards them, more as a gesture of grandiloquent contempt than anything else. Then I stumbled back into the shop feeling very sick.

Next evening I was walking along the High Street when I met the same youths again. They deliberately stretched themselves out to form a barricade on the pavement so that it was difficult for me to pass. I am built on something resembling the lines of a well-made tank so I kept on walking, looking neither to right nor left until they gave way and I was free to go on my way without further interruption.

'Why,' I thought, 'for all their big talk, they're really cowards.'

From that day I despised them, and I've never been frightened since. I hate brute force and I loathe foul language. I am not proud of the fact that I know that if the need had arisen I would have used my whip on them. Even if I had ended up in a police court, I don't think I should have minded. At least my action would have brought home to the police the possible awful consequences which could have upset a more elderly person than myself.

The incident depressed me. They were all so young. If they had to be so mean and moody at least let them be magnificent also.

Even the things that the beatniks and the ton boys profess to like are not safe from their tendency to enjoy destruction. Personally I have a liking for modern jazz, and when the Jazz Festival was first opened at Beaulieu I was delighted to go. The first time that I went it was a great pleasure to see so many young people enjoying themselves. They seemed so normal as they danced and laughed on the gracious lawns of the lovely old Palace House of Lord Montagu. Their applause of the fine musicians who gave a magnificent performance to provide amusement for them was an uplifting experience at that first Jazz Festival.

Then the year after, the beatniks and ton boys turned against the thing that they had seemed to enjoy. The destruction by hooligans at Beaulieu was a heartbreaking experience. Beneath the sloppy exterior of the students, the beatniks, the black-leather-coated ton boys, there is this sudden urge to destroy; a dormant savage instinct emerged at Beaulieu and it is a dangerous thing.

Suddenly some aspects of youth frighten me, it is a relief to know that at forty I am only an old square amongst the cool cats.

I wish I understood the cool cats better.

I look with relief at the innocence shown in a copy of a Reynolds portrait which hangs in the shop. It belongs to a different age and makes the painter fall into the same category as me. Just an old square.

14
Not for ever

ONE of the least happy aspects in the life of being an antique dealer is when I am called out to clear the remains of a broken home. Unfortunately, calls of this type have become much more frequent during the last few years. With all the benefits of our civilization there is the aftermath of unhappy human beings. After visiting a house where either a husband or wife is about to be engulfed in divorce proceedings, I find myself wondering how it all happened. What awful sets of circumstances result in the contents of a presumably once-happy home being transferred to my store-room? Too often an antique dealer such as myself sees more of the frailties and problems of human beings than even the solicitor involved in the case.

Not very long ago I went to the house of one of my most attractive customers. She was a well-groomed woman who had been married for many years to a man in a good position. They seemed to have everything necessary to contribute to a successful marriage. The woman was pleasing enough to catch the eye of any man, her husband was always pleasant and considerate to her when they came to the shop together. They had two nice children.

It was a shock to answer the 'phone one morning and hear a request to call at their house to buy 'everything'. I arrived at the address in a nearby seaside town to find that it was a flat, and I remembered being surprised even at that. Somehow I always associated them with a cottage in the country. The flat was neat and clean with just too much furniture.

Within a few minutes of entering the flat my client had begun to tell me the whole sordid tale. It had a familiar sound about it; not only had I heard it before but I had read of the same situation in a hundred books. I was told the name of the inevitable 'other woman' and again I felt a tremor of shock because I knew her as well. By a simple 'phone call, in the course of my ordinary round of work, I was being involved in a typical domestic triangle. It was like watching a stage play, but, in actuality, not one of the characters seemed real to me. The 'other woman' was not a *femme fatale* so beloved of the fiction writers. She was quite an ordinary young girl who worked in the same works as the husband. I am sure she had been engaged because of her neat appearance and nice manner in dealing with people.

From three quite ordinary people there was going to come the emotional tangle which could end up only in the divorce courts. The husband had left the house one day and eloped with the girl, leaving his wife distraught with their children. Something clicked in my brain and I remembered hearing a few days ago that this woman's husband had left his good safe job. Things were becoming clear.

As I listened to the wife telling me about the whole affair, I tried to distract my mind by viewing the meaningless panoply of this once happy marriage. As I packed the vases and bric-à-brac the wife kept up a constant diatribe against the 'other woman', punctuating the conversation with paroxysms of tears followed by a list of her own undoubted virtues.

'It isn't as if I haven't been a good wife to him,' she said. 'When we had nothing I loved him. I could never have left *him*.' Amazing though it may seem, it is a fact that many types of love will survive adversity only to become allergic to success. As I pondered on this, the wife went on, not because she wanted to talk to me so much as to herself. It was as if a frenzied reasoning force had to be released from her.

'I've been a good mother. Nothing has been too good for my children.'

It was the emphasis of 'my children' that upset me, not 'our children' but the unhappy possessive overpowering word 'my'. I was beginning to be frightened of the thoughts forming in my own mind. It was difficult to talk to her but I wanted her to take stock of herself. I let little prayers form in my mind. 'Think of one little fault in yourself,' I pleaded silently. This tragedy was not hers alone. If only she could think back in time to some moment when perhaps she had failed him I felt sure that it would help her. There must have been some moment when this *débâcle* of human happiness started, and when it could have been ended before it began. Perhaps there was some tiny moment when this good wife forgot to be a lover, when the mother instinct even made a thin dividing-line between her life and her husband's. How long ago did she begin to think of 'my children'? Was that the first haircrack in the fine porcelain quality of their brittle young lives?

We moved from the lounge to the bedroom and I could see two single beds. Cold, austere beds; how easy it must be to fall out of love. How easy for a simple marriage like this to go wrong, unless the wife is prepared to be part of the eternal sacrifice to the equally eternal needs of man.

Generally, when I am packing up a house, I can think only of the things that I am dealing with, but this time it was different. I was thinking all the time, but it was not about buying and selling. I fought against the desire to reason within myself about something which should be no concern to me, an antique dealer whose life is spent more in the shadows of the past than in the sunlight of the present. It was no good.

In the beginning of everything that has ever been, I could reason that there was only sex. A primeval instinct; savage, demanding but free from any frightening urge except that man must reproduce his species. From sex there came the by-product of love. A gentle reassuring balm against the savagery of sex. With civilization and man-made laws there came the contract of marriage. The legalization to produce progeny, and with marriage came complexity of living. If marriage is a contract then contracts can be made for so many things. For money, for improvement of position, for security and for love itself.

The wife talked and I packed. The wife talked and I thought. The process seemed to go on for a very long time.

I began to reason that most marriages fail for two main reasons;

sex or finance. In this household I sensed that it was not finance.
The husband had had a secure job earning good money but even
that could bring other problems.

Perhaps in his youth he had dreams of a different job, and in
order to give his wife security he gave up his dreams and took a
'good' job. With security there could come complacency. I could
see this little family being dragged into the treadmill of local
society. An eternal round of visiting friends with minute cocktail
parties and their pseudo air of conviviality. Little discussions
about other families. It could have been a world of ever-reducing
circles for this husband and wife.

I began to pack the books from the husband's bookcase and
noticed that they were all adventure stories. How much were these
books part of his real life? Was it from them that he sought the
adventures that would not come from his safe job? Did he ever
come home to anything more exciting than a carefully planned
fortnight's holiday? Did he scrimp and save to give the children
a good education and did he dream of holidays abroad? Nowadays,
with good working conditions, a man can be lulled into a feeling
of security. Yet perhaps he was bound far more securely himself,
more subtly but none the less bound. Only the outside of his life
needed to be different, the better home that he lived in than his
ancestors, the better education for his children than he had himself. These things can make a man forgo the natural instinct for
adventure.

Into the drabness of his security there had come the 'other
woman'.

I could not feel that the husband had left his wife without some
feeling of pain, there was too much of him left around the flat for
that. It was dreadful to know all the three points of the triangle.
I wanted to plan everything to come right but in my heart I knew
that it would not be so. In the meanwhile I, too, was embroiled
in the unhappiness and felt my own inadequateness to be helpful.

I knew that friends would offer every sympathy to the deserted
wife, a good family solicitor would smooth the path to the divorce
court.

There began to be a sense of indignation in me, and I was able to concentrate more on the packing of books, travel brochures, dress clothes, bric-à-brac. I told myself that I was an antique dealer and it was no fault of mine that I was forced into the role of overlooking the privacy of someone's life.

I threw the things which I had bought into the car, desperately anxious to get away to the inanimate object of my shop in the High Street. For once it seemed like a lifeline stretching out to me, and I wanted to grasp it so firmly that I could never escape from it again.

For once there had been nothing to laugh about in my visit to buy some things for the shop. For once, as I shut the door in the shop, I was relieved to be just an antique dealer again. The shop seemed kindly and sane that night. I had never thought of it before as a refuge for an escapist, for that is what I am when I return after a trip like that.

Next morning a dealer came and bought all the stuff which I had collected from the broken home. I let it be sold just as it stood, still in the packing-cases.

It was easier to forget the incident of being an unwilling on-looker into the secret recesses of the hearts of three people whom I would probably never see again.

The same set of circumstances would be reproduced again in the course of my life as an antique dealer. Only next time I would be prepared, and keep my mind on my work.

Too many close views of triangles would drive me mad. It's one thing to be zany but quite another to be mad!

15
Enter Adonis in search of a scalp

HE WAS young, virile, with the grace of a modern Adonis and he entered the shop looking as unhappy as any man could look. Yet it was spring and so many of our customers came into the shop to buy engagement rings. I summed this Adonis up as a potential buyer of some such trifle. He was so good-looking that it would be a pleasure to serve him. I saw myself picking out diamond-and-sapphire rings from the tray or possibly a Georgian amethyst surrounded by pearls; whatever he wanted we would most certainly exert ourselves to find something to please him. However, the suggestion of unhappiness on his face was disconcerting. After all, if he had come to buy an engagement ring, it would be surely a time for rejoicing. Why then this harassed look of utter weariness in the face of such a handsome man on whom nature had really gone to town to give him so much to make him look like Adonis?

As he stepped into the shop Mrs. Strong moved forward to meet him. It is not our policy to pounce upon customers as they set foot in the place, far from it. We love to let them potter around and enjoy themselves. No, it was spring, he was so terribly virile and handsome that there was every excuse to go half-way to meet him. I felt the urge to do so myself.

'Can I help you, sir?' said Mrs. Strong in her best rich contralto voice which always inspires confidence in the most nervous of customers.

I could hardly bear to wait to hear his voice. My fingers closed around the tattered jewellery-box where we keep our best bits of stuff. With a great finesse of timing, when Adonis spoke the magic words, I would flash open the jewel-box and produce a magnificent diamond-and-sapphire ring for his approval. I loved this particular ring myself but felt that it was waiting for some very special customer who would see it and love it. Who could be more special than this unknown Adonis?

'I don't suppose you can help me,' said Mr. Adonis, and now he looked quite pathetic in his extreme unhappiness. Like a man who has been searching a long time for something vital to his existence and is now facing up to the fact that he will never find it.

'We can try,' said Mrs. Strong, becoming sweetly maternal and oozing a tenderness which she reserves for the very young, the handsome, the gracious or the elegant ladies. (Far, far different from the way she treats me!)

'I wonder if you have . . .' He paused as if reluctant to voice his desires. I began to feel *de trop* but curiosity compelled me to stay.

'I wonder if you have . . . a long length of human hair?'

I slid the jewel-box quietly into the drawer of the desk, feeling a slight twinge of disappointment. Adonis could have asked for so many wonderful things, but 'a long length of human hair' . . . It brought a macabre touch which was out of place with the appearance of Mr. Adonis.

Mrs. Strong faltered, her eyes flickered uncertainly from Mr. Adonis to me as she always does when she senses anything unusual in the air. The time had come for me to step forward myself. I am a great believer in never appearing to be surprised at anything a customer may ask for.

'Have you any particular colour in mind, sir?' I asked, fearing in my heart that I was perhaps taking the matter a bit too far, but I wanted Adonis to feel more comfortable and optimistic than when he had entered the shop. I think my question gave him confidence because he turned eagerly towards me and smiled. The harassed look drifted away and his smile was in keeping with his fine Grecian features. He seemed to flounder a little at my questions.

'Well, I'd really settle for any length of human hair providing it is more than ten inches long, but what I really want, if I could choose, is a length of hair the colour of a Titian portrait.'

'Of course, sir,' I said smoothly, warming to the finer points of the subject myself. After all, a very Adonis probably dreams secret dreams of long lengths of Titian red hair. 'I think I have the very thing that you are looking for.'

'You have?' he replied, practically dehydrated with surprise. 'You really have such a thing, here, in this little shop?'

'If you can wait a few minutes whilst I go to get it, I am sure we can help you.' I put on my most calm efficient air. The worried look now went completely from his face leaving only his youth and handsomeness. 'Perhaps you would care to sit down and wait?'

Now my shop in the High Street has something of the quality of an iceberg in structure. About one-third of the goods which I own are actually on view to the public. It is a very small shop as viewed from the street, but beyond the shop we have treasures which have been unseen for many years, and underneath in the cellars are the other two-thirds of the iceberg—submerged. It is from this labyrinth that at times I can find something quite rare and unexpected.

I descended into the depths of the cellar, down the unsafe wooden steps, skipping lightly over the always present pool of water which lurks around the bottom. A sharp turn to the left brings me to a huge, iron-bound door. For our cellar in this quaint old building was originally the strong-room of one of the first banks in this town. Beyond the door in the actual strong-room we have a wonderful array of articles. I knew that somewhere in the chaos of dark dampness I had at one time put a tin box full of human hair, 'in a safe place'. I stood for a moment gazing at the things around me; thinking, thinking very hard of the place where I had cached it away. There are many chests of drawers and cupboards in the cellar to say nothing of trunks and boxes. On this particular day there were at least forty drawers inviting me to try them to see which one would contain the hair. In any one of them could lurk the long, long red tresses which would bring joy to the weary heart of Mr. Adonis. I desperately wanted to find the hair; the modest price that it would bring was nothing compared with the price I had anticipated obtaining by the sale of the sapphire ring, but I truly felt that the pleasure of Mr. Adonis would more than compensate me for the financial loss.

One of my few virtues is that I have a good memory for remembering where things are. I hoped that this was not going to be the time when I failed. To the eyes of a stranger our cellar is just a jungle of mysterious objects. I don't mind living in a state of chaos, it is only when Mrs. Strong tidies up that I am apt to lose track of things! If the muddle is of my own making there is a reasonable chance that I can track it down. I stood in the middle of jungle, thinking madly, and suddenly I remembered. I had put the hair in a tin biscuit-box, in a bottom drawer of a chest of drawers. Well, that eliminated the cupboards, anyway. I seemed to think back to a very large chest of drawers and that reduced the search even more. Finally I tossed up whether to try a large tallboy type of Victorian chest or a simply enormous mahogany one. I settled for the tallboy, only to be met with vexatious defeat. Then I turned my attention to the mahogany chest. The bottom drawer resisted my attack; I pulled and tugged but something had securely jammed it. This was not really surprising since every chest and every drawer in the entire place is crammed full of junk of some kind or other. I knew the hair was in this drawer and if I had to chop it open I intended to get it. I pulled, I tugged, I fell backwards as a handle came off. I kicked, coaxed, I swore. Finally, with the aid of a brass poker, I eased the thing that was stopping the drawer from opening and at last I pulled it out. The tin box was there; I opened it quickly to find the hair was indeed in it. After a moment to recover my breath from the exertions I marched triumphantly up the wooden steps back to the shop.

Mr. Adonis and Mrs. Strong were well away in an animated conversation about London and discovering that they knew Cadogan and Sloane Squares very well. It seemed quite cruel to interrupt them.

'Perhaps you would like to look at this, sir,' I said meekly, offering the tin box to Mr. Adonis. In the cold light of the day it looked revolting from the outside.

Mr. Adonis leaned forward and picked up the thick lengths of human hair. There were two full lengths; both had been tied at the top with neat and loving care. The tresses in his hand unfurled with languorous grace as he held them up. Now he was a different Adonis to the man who had come into the shop. He held it high up, his eyes flickered with approval, his other hand touched the hair caressingly.

'My God,' he said, practically choking with emotion, 'I would never have believed it possible. It's exactly what I've been looking for.'

I offered him the other length from the box. He took both so that they formed a quivering cascade of bright gold-red light. A waterfall of human hair shimmering in the pale sunlight. It fascinated us all. Mrs. Strong was as shaken as Mr. Adonis at the unexpected appearance of the hair. As for me, well, I knew that the time had come to reckon the hair in terms of money and it was not going to be easy. How can one translate into pound notes what the poets have always deemed 'a woman's crowning glory'? But it had to be faced and only I could do it.

'How much is it?' said Mr. Adonis.

'How much is it worth to you?' I parried quickly, wanting more time to think about it. Anyway, there was no need for him to be quite so blunt.

'Three pounds,' he said quickly. The Grecian nose seemed to have developed the slightest of hooks on it.

'Three pounds,' I said unbelievingly. 'For this, I hoped you would want *both* tresses.'

'I do,' said Adonis in surprise. 'I meant three pounds for the lot.'

'Oh, I am asking three pounds for one tress,' I said briskly. 'But, if you really want the lot, I'll tell you what I'll do. I'll let you have both lots for five pounds.'

There are times when I take my own breath away with sheer audacity. I held out my hand as if to take the hair away from him.

'Of course, if the hair is too much for you I don't mind keeping it. After all, it really is rather beautiful, so rare in colour don't you think? If you don't want it I can take it up to London with me next time I go. . . .'

After all, I had my losses to think about, and really he had no business entering my little shop on a spring morning looking like a possible customer for a sapphire ring and then asking for something which most shops would find it difficult to supply. I ignored Mrs. Strong's pleading looks and reminded myself to warn her not to be sentimental with good-looking customers in future.

Mr. Adonis scowled. That was his undoing. When he scowled he became only as other men. A scowl is never becoming and even an Adonis can't hope to get away with it. I don't like good-looking men who spoil things by scowling. I decided not to weaken.

'Five pounds,' I said firmly, clicking the lid of the tin suggestively against the box, giving the impression that I had very little more time to waste.

'Oh, well,' he said ungraciously, 'I'll have them both.' He flicked his hand into his pocket and drew out a five-pound note. Really the Adonis of today is not as gracious as one could wish, but the fiver looked a good one so I took it calmly and nonchalantly fluttered it into the drawer which we use as a till.

'Thank you so much, sir,' I smiled sweetly. 'Mrs. Strong will wrap it up for you.'

He handed the hair to Mrs. Strong as if he hated to part with it for a moment. She packed it with the same sure, deft touch which she uses when she packs some fragile piece of porcelain.

I opened the door for him, smiling brightly as he passed from the shop into the High Street. A girl in the fish shop smiled at him but he walked past her. A tall, very handsome man clutching a little parcel of human hair of Titian red.

'I wonder what he wanted it for?' asked Mrs. Strong.

I looked at her in surprise.

'Surely you asked him when I was in the cellar?'

'No,' she said plaintively. 'We just talked about London.'

I felt slightly cross, for I too wanted to know what he wanted the hair for!

We have never seen him again. I like to think of him being in London, very happy with the long tresses of some unknown woman near to him.

He was such a nice young man.

'He must be mad,' I said to Mrs. Strong. 'Going around asking in shops like ours if we have long lengths of human hair. Titian red indeed!'

'Is he?' said Mrs. Strong. 'Perhaps he thinks you're mad, too. After all, you've kept it hidden away long enough here. . . .'

Really, this manageress of mine says the strangest things at times. After all, I bet everyone really keeps two lengths of human hair in Titian red in a chest of drawers in the cellar. You never know when a thing may come in handy and give a wealth of pleasure to someone else, do you?

He was a nice young man; we often talk about him.

I wonder who *she* was, the woman whose red hair ended up in the cellar of a shop in a High Street? I am quite sure she would have liked our Mr. Adonis.

16
Fresh flowers today, lady?

ONE of the most pleasant women who come into the shop is the gypsy woman who brings my flowers every Wednesday and Saturday. She is called Rose. Many Romany families favour the names of flowers for their children. I know one family whose register of offspring reads like a garden manual. Pansy, Primrose, Lilac, Daffy, Lily, Petunia, Poppy and such names. I suppose it is natural for people who live close to nature to have a preference for the simple names rather than adopt the more exotic Moiras and Brigittes which seem to be popular amongst the children of the Gorgios.

My Rose as she walks down the High Street with her enormous basket of flowers is a pleasure to see. She is tall for a gypsy woman, with an oval face and high cheekbones. She cannot be very young in years, but she is always as sprightly as a sparrow. Her black hair is worn in thick braids wound around each ear, the traditional hair style for the old-school gypsies. Full golden hoop ear-rings swing beneath the dark hair and, because the flower trade is good, she can always manage to keep her fingers covered in good, old-fashioned gold rings. I do not think I have ever seen her with less than five rings. She comes to Ringwood twice a week in all weathers. Her polite manner, even to the odd customer who decides not to buy her flowers, is an example to any shopkeeper.

When she arrives in Ringwood with her home-made basket filled brimful with the particular flowers of the season she comes first of all to me in the shop. When the wild daffodils are in season, the gold basket gleams like sunshine against the greyness of the street. In summer she sells a motley collection of flowers, but she always tells me that it is the autumn that she likes best. For then she comes with tawny chrysanthemums.

As Christmas approaches the Butcher's Broom of the Forest is cut and twisted with home-made wax flowers, a foil for the unreal waxen beauty of Christmas roses.

Rose has her regular customers in Ringwood; many hoteliers buy from her. At noon she walks down the High Street again but this time the basket is filled to the brim with groceries. In return for her trip to Ringwood after a full day's work at home in cutting and arranging the flowers she has substituted the less romantic goods needed to feed her large family. The prices that she asks for her flowers are so low that I marvel how she can manage to buy so many groceries.

One day Rose came in to me whilst I was in the middle of a bad attack of asthma and coughing my head off.

She looked at me with great sympathy in her brown eyes. 'You'm bad today, missus,' she said.

I nodded, having no breath left to reply. She left the shop, to my surprise without even giving me the chance to choose any flowers. Within an hour she was back and handed me a small envelope containing a red, crudely ground powder.

'You take this, missus,' she said.

I gathered that it must be some sort of medicine but in my face I must have shown some doubt, for she went on:

'It won't kill ye afore the cough gets yer.'

Gingerly I put a pinch of the red powder in my mouth whilst Rose looked quite pleased. I swallowed the stuff, thinking that anyway one can die only once. It was like swallowing balls of fire. I dared not cough in case I went up in flames. Through watering eyes I could see Rose's face crinkling into smiles.

'You'll be worse before you'm better.'

I knew I couldn't feel worse than this; the balls of fire had reached my stomach; there they must have died away for suddenly I felt much better.

'What on earth have you given me?' I asked.

''Tis good stuff. My uncle was once taken like you and I gave him this. Benny took it all the way to Sommyset and he was right as rain afterwards. Lived to be seventy but he allus tuk his red powder.'

It seemed very reassuring. I hoped that Uncle and I had enough in common to share the same beneficial results.

'You keep the rest o' they powder, missus. When you'm had it, I'll give you some more.'

I realized that she meant this kindly but the thought of having periodical doses of burning fire poured into me was rather frightening. Anyway, I hid the powder. Whatever it was, it seemed to do me good, for I did not cough any more and seemed to breathe more easily. Perhaps it was imagination, but the resultant feeling was good enough for me.

Rose sold me some flowers. Tactfully I offered her some money for the powder but she would not take it. No one will ever tell me that gypsies are greedy, grasping creatures who are always wanting money. They know there is a time for such things but this was not Rose's way to make money. Knowing the way in which gypsies love presents I resolved to give her something from the shop when next she came in. But I badly wanted to know what the red powder was, I felt I owed it to my stomach to get the name in order to make a proper introduction.

At the end of the week Rose popped into the shop in her usual way and asked how I felt. She didn't seem surprised when I said I felt wonderful.

'Come on,' I said. 'Do tell me what the red powder is?'

' 'Tis nothing more than they little red pods me parrot has,' she said seriously.

I felt stupefied.

'Red pods' indeed!—she'd given me ground-up chillies! I doubt if she bought them specially for medicinal purposes. I could well imagine her just whipping a few from the bottom of the parrot cage and I practically saw myself dead of that disease with an unspellable name which makes headlines in the papers from time to time. A fine thing to be cured of asthma only to gain parrot disease! Rose laughed when I told her, quite gaily.

'You'm live,' she said. Well, I'm still alive and I had that first dose three years ago. I must admit that I keep the red powder in my desk, but I buy the chillies myself. No sense in asking for trouble. Many people laugh at the remedies that gypsies give for various ailments but they keep reasonably well themselves even though they live in conditions which are ripe for producing diseases. Once, when I was at an old farmhouse I saw a gypsy trap his hand in a car door. It looked an awful mess. He looked at it ruefully but ran off into the cowhouse; I followed him in to see if I could help him but he had only gone to the cowhouse for his 'remedy'. He wrapped an enormous cobweb from the cowhouse around his hand whilst I watched in fascinated amazement. Next market-day I saw him buying horses in the top market and asked how his hand was. He appeared to have forgotten the accident.

'Why, 'tis better,' he said. 'They old cobwebbies be real good for anything like that.'

A week ago the hand had been mangled and inflamed. Today it was slightly swollen and pinkish but not causing him any discomfort.

How can you argue against their own medicine when it seems to work? Is it just a matter of faith? I don't know and probably never will but it works, this crude application of family remedies for various accidents and ailments.

I can understand how people like Rose like to use the natural herbs of the country, and she often tells me that she sometimes goes out to collect herbs for a man living in Southampton. They seem to have arranged their own health service to their satisfaction, these Romany friends of mine. I never hesitate to use any of the herbs that Rose brings even if sometimes I do not know their name, but she can generally tell me what they are good for.

Unfortunately the use of herbs these days seems to make one into a crank, but I know from personal experience how valuable these simple remedies can be. I have many friends who suffer from that strange thing called migraine. A painful complaint which does not seem to respond to orthodox medical treatment. Yet to rest quietly in a darkened room with the head on a pillow of fragrant if nameless herbs can give relief where more complicated treatment fails.

It is too easy really, and one can hardly go around recommending herbs when there are so many nice doctors anxious to earn a living on the Health Service. Besides, the recitation of symptoms and ailments can fill in many an odd moment in a village tea party. It is perhaps a little old-fashioned these days to be just plain healthy, as Rose appears to be. There are so many intriguing ailments available with interesting and impressive names that it would be a shame to cure them too simply.

During the many years that Rose has come to my shop to sell her flowers I have never known her to be ill. When the rest of the world is suffering from Asian, Spanish or plain English flu, Rose strolls through the High Street without the suspicion of a sniffle. I asked her one day if she ever had a cold.

'I reckon I'm healthy 'cos I don't live in a house,' she said quite seriously. 'I sleeps in the old wagon and I spends all me day out in the air.'

'Were you born in a wagon?' I asked curiously.

'Oh no,' said Rose. 'Me folks were tenting people but I married right and we'm got our own wagon.'

I knew that Rose felt that she had gone up in her social status. To be born into one of the old tenting families who drift around the Forest must surely be the hardest form of all gypsy life. In the old days it was the tenting women who gave birth to their children under the shelter of the hedges. They returned to the fragile shelter of the tent only when the child was safely born in order to cause little disturbance as possible to the family life. Rose, with her cheerful face and simple philosophy for living, could not have had an easy childhood. Yet somehow she had survived and was well enough to enjoy the Forest in all its seasons.

A friend of mine recently painted Rose and her daughters, each holding their big baskets brimful of flowers. I bought the picture, and within eighteen hours I had sold it.

A lady driving through the town on her way to Bournemouth saw the picture in the window. She parked the car and came to the shop to enquire the price. The sale was completely painless, and as she was making out the cheque I could not stop myself from asking her why she had decided to buy this particular picture.

'They look so happy,' she said. 'When this picture is in my room I think I shall be able to share their happiness and feel I have a part of the Forest with me.'

It seemed a good enough reason for anyone to buy the picture and I felt pleased that it would live with someone who appreciated it. It was a pleasure to me to sell a painting like this, which depicted only happiness in a simple form. So many times I have to steel myself to sell a picture which shows probably some deep and subtle meaning. Alas, the meaning is often obscure and must remain a secret for ever with the artist who painted it, it fails to communicate with the person looking at it. I felt something of the sentiment of the lady who bought the painting of a few simple Forest flower-girls. For when I buy my flowers from Rose I know that I am not buying only two-shillings' worth of flowers. I feel as if I am buying a share in their lives and something of their happiness is transmitted to me. I know I pay too little for my flowers.

17
God bless our American cousins

FROM May until September the giants of the shipping world plying between New York and Southampton spill out their passengers who spread out across England on a cultural tour, or perhaps only a business tour. For antiques in America are really *big*, Big Business. My best clients arrive at the shop regularly with a chauffeur, a secretary and a representative of a shipping firm in London who will deal with the ultimate despatch of any antiques purchased. There is nothing trivial to their approach to buying— they are here with the firm intention of doing business; they have travelled a long way to do it, and if they can buy from you then they are happy.

They come armed with knowledge but with strangely conservative tastes. They know exactly what the American public will buy next year and nothing will divert them into trying something new. It's toast-racks, entrée dishes in Sheffield or silver, or nothing. It's four-piece tea-sets and on no account will they take a three-piece set, in silver or plate. It's Georgian silver, coloured Victorian glass, fine furniture or English homestead furniture, and they will take it by the hundred if you have the lines they happen to deal with. In my time I have supplied copper kettles by the hundred, whilst commodes of all shapes and sizes are my present 'big' line. I have a client who will take *any* amount of commodes. If I could only offer him a choice bargain in Sutherland tables, but it wouldn't mean a thing to him; at the moment he is selling commodes and that's that. So for the next six months at least I have commodes in every conceivable place in my house and as I write we are stacking them four high in the store-room. A drop in the commode market in America would make me the biggest collector of commodes probably in the world! What a dreadful thought!

Anything in natural pine is another favourite 'buy' for certain Americans. I believe this fits very well into the New England type of house. Fortunately, I have a client who does not mind taking it in the rough, for if you have tried cleaning stain, muck and dirt of ages off a pretty pine cupboard, then you know what real work is! Personally, the plain, scrubbed-table look of pine does not appeal to me but it *sells*, and as long as America buys it I'll find it and sell it.

Another American buyer of mine deals only in ornate bedroom ware—sets of ewers and basins with chambers and pails are his pride and joy. I never realized that the Victorian bedroom ware was so attractive until I began to go 'chamber-spotting' on behalf of this client. It was certainly an education. Some of the truly magnificent pieces had enormous footbaths in a set, and these fetch some interesting prices. All the big potteries did bedroom ware, and they combined good workmanship and delightful designs on many pieces.

The American buyers come in all sizes but can roughly be divided into the willing, happy type of buyer and the antagonistic and frighteningly national type who thinks England is rather a dump but is all right for buying antiques. They imply that it takes an American home to show them off to the best advantage and that the American way of mucking around with perfectly good antiques shows a rare type of initiative. Such as making perfectly good English Georgian silver soup-ladles into cute, modern American ashtrays to sling over armchairs. I think that when I first heard about this I was more appalled than by anything else. Since then I've really never had the heart to deal in soup-ladles. It seems a much lesser evil to use toast-racks for letter-racks, at least it is a painless and even reasonable progress of rehabilitation.

With the advent of the serious although often one-track-minded Americans, there also come the American tourists. To them, visiting antique shops is part of the 'tour' and probably acts as a form of higher education. One visualizes them solemnly receiving a Certificate of Merit, showing that they have served an apprenticeship period of antique-spotting all over England. Certainly if small shops like mine had to rely on the American *tourist* trade we should be in very sorry straits. Being mindful of upholding American friendship in this troubled world of political unrest, I work on a policy of being desperately nice as my small personal contribution to world peace. But, dearie me, the going is made very hard, particularly when the tourist adopts a most patronizing air, and I can imagine her writing home at night to 'Paw' in Pennsylvania:

'Dear Paw,
        This day we visited an antique shop in little old Ringwood. We established friendly relations with the natives by trading them a few beads; the natives appear to be harmless and not of a cannibalistic nature.
                    Your affectionate Daughter of the Revolution,
                    Mamie Veutwanger-Dobbs. . . .'

Still, the tourists do not arrive unexpectedly. They are purely seasonal and one can therefore take precautionary measures. Every American tourist who comes to my Ringwood shop is either just off the boat at Southampton and faced with a journey of thousands of miles around England and is reluctant to spend any money at the first drop of their suitcase or, alternatively, they are doing the trip in reverse and are hieing wearily back to catch a boat at Southampton 'that very night' and have only a few cents left to see them to the boat. Dreamily, I hope one day to find a shop plumb centre of the American Grand Tour, for surely there must be *some* place where they go mad and really *buy* things. Sister—that place is sure not Ringwood!

So for my part I concentrate on the American 'dealing' types, the wholesale buyers from Douglasville, Baltimore, Connecticut, Philadelphia and good old New York. I like their singleness of purpose, the impulse that sends a man thousands of miles to buy hundreds of just one commodity. I wonder what a man feels who only buys commodes for ever and ever, month after month? I foresee great advertising campaigns, saying: 'No American household is complete without a Georgian commode. Get *yours* now, whilst stocks, from Leek's of Ringwood, last.'

It is as puzzling to me as American politics. I guess even today I'll never know whether it's Republicans or Democrats who buy my commodes, or is this the point when they drop party politics and become as one, united by the love of one of Leek's famous commodes?

I feel that this is a mellow note to think of our American cousins, God bless them, one an' all!

18
I remember her
when she hadn't a penny

THE window of our shop in the High Street is truly enormous. It rises as a solid sheet of glass from within a few inches of the footpath to perhaps ten feet or more. It is infinitely more than ten feet when I clean it, for it is a glorious old-fashioned waterfall of a window. On the pavement, perhaps drawn by the objects in the window or because of the sparkling lustrous lights of the chandeliers, we always have a bevy of ladies gossiping outside our window. Without wishing to eavesdrop at all, it is inevitable that we should hear some quite strange subjects as topics of conversation. We have our regular gossipers, of course, and on Tuesdays in particular we wait for our favourite trio who, at the moment, are giving us a recital of their love life in weekly serial form. It is quite as interesting as *The Archers* and I can't bear to miss a word of it. But in five weeks we have not yet learnt who the gorgeous 'he' is. I wish I knew, for nothing in Ringwood would seem to be quite so wonderful as this mysterious, unknown 'he'. I personally think he is a bus conductor but my manageress says no, he is something on the council. Anyway, I give them till Easter to announce the wedding day!

However, it is a true saying the eavesdroppers never hear any good of themselves. One day two local ladies were looking in the window and eyeing me vaguely at the same time. In a clear English voice I distinctly heard one say, 'Of course, I remember *her* when she hadn't a penny to her name.' A brief conversation followed which distinctly points to the fact that the 'her' in this conversation was *me*!

It was a fairly busy morning for me and it was not until lunchtime that I really began to consider her remark, and to realize how true it was. The unfortunate and very sad thing about it was that I, too, remember with horrifying vividness the days when I hadn't a penny to my name. It is a feeling that will always be with me, of walking down this High Street with exactly eight and sixpence in the world.

The street was full and of all the people there was no one in this town who gave a tinker's cuss that someone walked in stricken panic in the High Street.

I walked the whole length of the town that day, slowly taking in every little thing that I saw. Loving it as if I was never to see it again, for somehow I felt that there was nothing left to live for, that there was no life left in me. My whole past life was shed with each step that I took round that town. It was September, a terrible, soul-destroying September, and yet for me the complete turning-point in a most tempestuous life. On that day—I died. No one saw it, no one wanted to know, but the thing that had been me was gone. And for this very reason I call all my businesses by the name of 'Phoenix', because I know now there is really no death. Only the terrifying pangs of rebirth as one passes from one phase of life to another. Phoenix—a new life arising from a holocaust of disaster, a burning-up of one thing to form another. In my case the Phoenix at the moment is a bit flamboyant, but its feet still rest on that day not so long ago when I, too, remembered that I hadn't got a penny.

Madam, it was not necessary to remind me. Everything I do in my present life is calculated to remind me of that. Every sale I make is an insurance against dying again in this High Street. Once, in a day of mad braggadocio, after pulling off a really exciting big sale, I walked again the whole length of Ringwood, this time with real money in my pocket, but I was not thinking of that; I was living with every step the moments of that other day in September, almost so intense was the feeling that I was transported back in time. Then I remembered the wealth in my wallet and I took it out in the High Street under the glare of a street lamp and shouted with sheer uninhibited laughter.

There was not a soul in sight, and there was again the aloneness in myself, whether I have eight and sixpence in my purse or a fortune, a terrible aloneness.

There is no virtue in poverty, no taste in nothing and, paradoxically, no meaning in wealth, no love in success. Yet the poverty, nothingness, a taste of wealth and even of success are now all equal parts of my make-up.

There is a quotation from 'Dante's Inferno' which I often think about: 'There is no greater misery than remembering past times of great happiness.'

Equally so there is no greater happiness than in remembering past times of great misery and knowing that they are over. So, dear ladies who gossip in front of my window, when you are 'remembering *her* when she hadn't got a penny' I shall be remembering with you, for ever and ever. It is not the successes of life that are important, these I *can* forget, but the soul-scarring failures are with me for always and have given me an armour in which I can cope with life and living.

Because 'I remember when I hadn't a penny to my name', each day is now the beginning of an adventure in which it is a sin to be unhappy for very long.

By the same measure, I now love *people* for their imperfections rather than for their virtues. In short, I am in love with humanity; its frailness, its struggles, its pathos and its resilience. The age-old triumph of life over death.

19
A deal in a field

ONE of the quickest and happiest sources of finance in the small market town antique shop is the sale of copper and brass. It appeals to many people not only on the grounds of age but for its purely utilitarian qualities. It is also very pleasant in any household on the long winter evenings to see the coal in a mellow, helmet-shaped copper coal-scuttle whilst the firelight plays tricks on the patina of a brass fender and fire-irons. To find things like this and maintain a constant supply of them so that people can come to the shop and know that you will always have something in copper and brass to offer them needs quite a lot of organization. The most effective way, which has proved itself satisfactory to me, is to buy from the travellers who roam the areas of the New Forest. They have a flair for finding things of a metallic nature and I have had some wonderfully interesting things from the Romanies of the area. It is a matter of pride to me that I know practically every travelling family in this region, and that they never fail to visit me whenever they are passing my shop. Sometimes it is purely for business, sometimes only for a 'dicker'. I never disguise the fact that I like travellers, they bring a dash of colour with them. Their history is one of persecution, as is that of the Jews, and whilst as a race the Romanies are perhaps not quite so intelligent, at least they merit a better fate than to be constantly hustled from one place to another as they are at the moment. Justice does not exist as far as Romanies are concerned in the New Forest; they are 'moved on' *before* they commit any crime other than offending some V.I.P. by their very presence. The sight of Romanies starting to camp in a pathetic bit of woodland immediately makes all the telephones in the area start to ring with fearful messages to the local police force—'Clear these people away'! Such is the promptness of the local police in dealing with Romanies that they have been known to arrive at an encampment before a match has been put to the fire. Their devotion to duty is highly commendable, but on the occasion when I was being menaced by a crowd of hooligans in my own shop I was told the police could do nothing, as 'no one had hurt me yet'. No, there is no justice for Romanies, only the drone of 'move on, move on' in monotonous repetition, year in, year out.

True there are difficult travellers. Much is made of the fact that they fight, but there is rarely any viciousness in them unless provoked beyond human endurance. The travellers who call on me are by no means a virtuous lot but we understand each other very well. To begin with I have no sentimental approach to Romanies. To me they are simply *people* following a way of life which I must not condemn because it varies from my own. As with the colour question, people in this area are either violently anti-Romany or of the rather sickly, artistic type who think them quaint. Romanies tolerate me chiefly because I give no quarter in dealing with them. This they respect. I, too, have my status to think of when bargaining with them and it is a matter of pride to 'come off best'! This bargaining can be done so that everyone enjoys themselves and in the end no face is lost by anyone. I learnt my dealing ways with Romanies the hard way, from the days when I was a female horse-dealer (plus goats and dogs), and if you can deal with Romanies in horses, and still make money, then you have served a good apprenticeship. No one comes to me now with the whining air that all Romanies adopt when mongering. Every deal takes an age to complete because time is as nothing to travelling folk. There are stories to be told, news of other families to be discussed, enquiries about each other's businesses (to the latter question we both lie abominably; each knows the other is lying so there is no harm done!). After all this there is the real thing to be discussed. They have copper pans to sell, and know I want to buy. The art of finding the right degree where the pans become my possession and no one's sense of fair play is outraged—ah, that is a brilliant technique, a joy of bargaining which the ordinary 'shopkeeper' will never know. So the Romanies say, 'Oh, Missus Silvie, her be a rare dealing woman. . . .' Why the old ones call me 'Silvie' or 'Silver' I'll never know, but names are as nothing to the travelling folk. Perhaps the 'Silver' comes about because in the old, old days I had a passion for buying all light-coloured horses—silvers, dapples, pied and/or any 'right coloury horse'.

News travels fast amongst the travellers. Once the news got about that I was in the market for copper they came, with the dirty coal-scuttles, the old paraffin lamps, the brass *jardinières,* the candlesticks. Of all shapes, sizes and vintage they came. Sometimes rubbed up until they shone, but mostly 'in their natural'. As one family moves on to Kent or Somerset, I'll swear that they 'bequeath' me to other relatives who are moving in! Certainly I am never without my clan of Romany scouts.

Not all my deals with travellers take place in the shop itself. The best and certainly the happiest have been in places where the hard, made-up council roads become green paths and trees take the place of cement lamp standards. In driving wind and rain I have stood in fields or in the woodlands and more money has changed hands on these occasions than has ever been done in the shop. This is the time when I know that at heart I am a *dealer*, not a shopkeeper, a 'buyer of things' rather than a seller of commodities. I do not long only to sell fine antiques. There are times when it is a holiday for me to do a deal in a field, whether it is for a load of old scrap-iron or for fifty street lamps or even for a trailer caravan. The incongruity of it touches off a slightly twisted sense of humour in me. Have a hundred ounces of Georgian silver in the back room, take it to the elegant salons of London, enjoy the sophistication of a day in Town, eat a fabulous lunch in Soho, buy the whole of a flower-seller's basket of flowers for the fun of it. Then, the next day, walk into the Forest to meet some travellers, buy copper pans and garden seats. Eat bread-and-cheese and drink the strong, black, sickly-sweet tea so beloved of the travellers. Both days have their merit but it is the fusion of both days that give my life in the High Street an extra zest and a full sense of the *joie de vivre* which might otherwise be difficult to attain.

With the old Romany travellers there also comes the show people and the circus folk. If you strip away the pseudo glamour from these people, and view them quite free of sentimentality, then you are able to assess them fairly. Beneath the dirt and the squalor of circumstances you find only *people*, like you and me. They have vices and virtues, so have you and I, but so often their vices are the product of the environment which we, the virtuous ones, have created for them. The 'phone call which brings a policeman at the double to say 'Move on' covers a myriad of the sins of civilization. Whenever I see a pathetic brood of travellers stamping out their fires and preparing to take to the road again I see the same resigned look which I saw on the columns of Jews being shuttlecocked through Europe. The sharp pain in my own heart makes me forget my shop in the High Street and for a little moment their burden is mine. I have seen it before, and any state of affairs that brings this look to the face of a human being is wrong, and even more wrong in England, the so-called fair land of the free. We open up our country to refugees from other lands yet we have our own problem of practically 'stateless' people, the Romanies, who have been here for many generations, a wandering people, *of* us, but not yet a part; a truth which we deny because they have not been assimilated into our standard of conformity. Truth must indeed be for ever buried into the deepest wells when our system of law and order chooses to ignore the existence of a *race*. Oh, what a beautiful amiable ostrich is the Englishman! He works passionately with his wife on committees for refugee funds and church missions, but an English-born Romany at the bottom of his garden makes him shake with self-righteous indignation, in *anticipation* of crimes not yet committed! I do not mean, either, that every English family should take a Romany into the bosom of its family. *They* don't want to intrude into your life but they *do* want the tolerance to lead their own life. To pitch a van in the forest for a night or two; to trade in tin and other metals. To flaunt their horses and perhaps do a deal with a 'l'il old pony, as dee and quiet as you like'. Within a day or two they would move on because it is in their nature to do so. All the Romany asks from the Gorgio (and that means *you*) is tolerance. And what is tolerance but the basic quality of every religion in the world. Poor old tolerance and truth; they get a thin time in this rough old civilization of ours! If truth is in a well, then tolerance has yet to be born!

To me, the happiest deals I have had have been in the fields, free from the stifling depression of commercialism, far from the nerve-shattering whine of a telephone and where no contract is ever needed beyond a man's word and a shake of the hand. For these moments of freedom from the panoply of Big Business are the moments to be thankful for. I have entered a world that is not mine but no man has shouted: 'Stranger, move on! Move! Move on!'

20

Fun and games
around the countryside

MANY of my acquaintances often appear to be shocked that once upon a time I earned the major part of my living by being a 'knocker'. This means that I used to go around the countryside from door to door asking if anyone had any silver or gold or jewellery for sale. Or indeed anything else for that matter. I see nothing degrading in this any more than it goes against the social grain to sell goods from a private house. Going on the knocker may even be a tiny bit more honest, for people know that you are out to earn a living this way, although I am sure it is not so pleasant as dealing with one's friends. I know from personal experience that it is not an easy way to earn a living, although I can look back now and even laugh about that period of my life. Today, I think I would be too soft to do it. Certainly it takes the urge of necessity and a lot of courage to go on the knocker. The measure of success in my own life is that now I can choose to do the things that I want to do without the grinding hardship of necessity to drive me on. Or maybe as my youthful energy has dwindled so has my courage!

Once upon a time I had some shockingly brilliant yellow papers printed.

WANTED   WANTED   WANTED

HAVE YOU ANY OF THE UNDERMENTIONED ITEMS THAT YOU WISH TO DISPOSE OF?

Silver and silver-plated items
China, Porcelain and glass

Antique Jewellery
Clocks and Watches
Copper and Brass
Staffordshire or similar figures
Garden Ornaments and Garden furniture
Anything in Wrought iron
Antique Furniture of any period, including Victorian
Gold and Silver Coins
Vintage Cars
Anything odd or unusual
Bric-a-brac
Oil paintings and miniatures

A buyer able to offer the highest prices will be at
. . . .
. . . .
on
. . . .

The impact of these well-distributed leaflets resulted in some fabulous feats of buying! I know that some of the London dealers work by this method. A buyer for a big firm takes a room at possibly a Bournemouth hotel and indicates by an advertisement in the local press that he will be available at room Y at X hotel to buy diamond rings, etc. I have tried this, but on a smaller scale, of course. There have been moments—and far too many of them —when buying just one very small insignificant diamond ring could have eaten up all my limited capital.

By a process of trial and error I evolved a satisfactory means of working in the country. First of all I would decide on an area to 'work up'. The choice of area was often decided whilst I was prowling around the countryside by car. The deciding factor of location had to take in the amount of big houses in the area. A country place with a hinterland of fine old houses, preferably a good few miles from any town, I have always regarded as my ideal. For everyone in a big, rambling type of house has something that they do not want and such houses also cost a lot of money to maintain. The percentage of owners who are glad to have a little extra easily earned ready money is therefore greater. Mushroom communities of bungalows or places with a large preponderance of council houses are no good for a good buying-spree.

The occupants of large houses, miles away in the country away from shops, do not always want to look out their surplus goods to take personally into an antique shop. A knock on the door or a discreet putting through the letter-box of one of my famous yellow papers jogs their memory into thinking that the jumble in their attic could be turned into money. They will make the effort to do this whilst they would not see the thing through to the bitter end by loading stuff into their car to trail round to an antique shop. They may choose just the wrong shop or a day when the owner is not thrilled at the idea of buying any more goods, and such car trips can deteriorate into bad temper for both parties. It is much better to be able to go to a house or be available in the area to buy.

The joy of my life when I was on the knocker was to be allowed to go into people's attics and clear all the stuff away myself. The owners had the minimum of work and I had the maximum amount of profit, so that left us both happy. In the course of a few months on the knocker I became an absolute expert on attics in many country areas. Some of my best 'buys' have been from attics. Once I bought the entire contents of a shockingly dirty attic for twenty-five pounds. The owner was delighted to have it cleared. It was so dark and miserable that I could not fully assess how much stuff was in the place at the first visit. I paid the twenty-five pounds cheerfully enough but it took me two full days to clear it. When the stuff reached my store-room (in the days when I was on the knocker a decrepit, disused, large poultry-house was called the 'store-room') I began to sort it out. My first real find was an old suitcase with the hinges rusted with age, so that I had to hack through the case to get at the contents. Inside was a collection of Victorian stamps including about 300 of the five-shilling ones. To this day I am still sorting through stamps in my spare time, although I sold many of them immediately. An enormous Victorian trunk made of cane, with a rounded top, yielded many period costumes of most beautiful design and workmanship. Many of these went to a museum as well as to a dealer in period costumes, and the not quite so interesting ones went to the local dramatic society. I frequently have the pleasure of seeing these used for such period pieces as *The Ideal Husband*.

Oh, that was an attic to think about with affection! . . . I could bear the moth-eaten rubbish in some of the other boxes just for the sake of the stamps and the costumes alone. Life was exciting and full of promise after such a buy as this but the joy was only too often shortlived, for possibly the next half-dozen attics would yield a sordid accumulation of old beds and worthless things. There were many days when all I got were corns on my knuckles with knocking at doors and hard skin on my feet with walking many unproductive miles—to say nothing of the unseen scars on my mind after a series of snubs and rudeness at a good many doors.

If you aren't tough when you go on the knocker you certainly are when you retire—if you survive, that is.

It was much easier to work from a hotel room or from the local pub. I used to send out my yellow papers and then take a room at the nearest central 'local'. At first I used to take a lot of reading matter to while away the long periods between visitors. During one quiet period I once taught myself the rudiments of Italian sufficient to be able to read newspapers in the language, as well as being able to converse reasonably well. But periods like this always fretted me. I was not in the country to improve my mind but to earn some money. Fortunately the Italian learning period soon passed. Trade became brisk and even in some of the most isolated pubs I discovered that life could be quite hectic. That was the way I liked my fun and games in the country.

The essential asset for dealing from a pub or hotel is always to have a few hundred pounds of hard cash available. Only real money in the shape of pound notes and fivers will register results for country people. Offer a cheque and they think that they are going to be taken for a ride. I am always amazed that country people have suspicious natures and know all the sordid tricks for being twisted. They always seem to have the idea in the back of their mind that a newcomer to their village is out to 'do' them. Personally, I think it would take a 'good one' to twist a country type. I have always enjoyed my expeditions into the country, not merely because they have been profitable but because they have been the means of meeting interesting people.

I always wondered what the recipients thought when they received one of my yellow invitations to sell goods. I never knew this and it was tantalizing, but I did know how people made the first approach.

The arrogant types sent the maid or gardener to the pub where I was staying, with a note requesting me to call at a precise time. Humbly I obeyed. Sometimes I was greeted as if I had come to collect the refuse and at times like this firmness on my part was essential. I always deducted something from the original price I offered for goods if the seller was bad-mannered. It didn't serve any more useful purpose than help me regain my own confidence, I had no time for haughty, aristocratic types with bad manners; generally I discovered that they were people who had lived abroad and were used to having native servants around. Because I was free, white and over twenty-one I had the choice of retaliation, which resulted in not being able to buy anything. Or I could be as hard as nails, using my own skill as a buyer to compensate me for receiving insults. Generally the sellers, however top-drawer they might be, once they had invited me to the house were extremely keen to sell, and even if every deal could not be done under ideal conditions I had to be thankful for small mercies. Dealers can't be choosers and it was better to let my mind remain on one thing only. To buy and to buy well enough to make a thumping good profit. After all, it wasn't a social occasion.

However, I must admit that if I have a sentimental spot in

my heart at all it is apt to come out when dealing with old people. I have seen so many financial tragedies connected with old age. Elderly ladies who could not face going into a shop to sell their belongings have always come to me at my room in the hotel. Always they bring small trinkets, and always there is a story to go with the trinkets. A little gold Victorian heart-shaped charm suddenly becomes important; a personal link between the seller and myself. Conversation sends the seller back to dreaming of her youthful days, when perhaps the pretty gold charm was a present from a dead husband who was then a lover. My cynical old heart gives a lurch and I kid myself that for a gold charm which has a story the price must be a little more than for a gold trinket alone. It is only when I arrive back in my shop that I know that only the charm can be sold and not the story, and I am back to reality again.

So I become a feminine edition of a modern Robin Hood; penalizing bad manners and arrogance in order to pay inflated prices for a gold charm! Logically I ought never to be a business woman if old people can make my heart play ducks and drakes with my business sense. Yet I don't know. It seems to have worked out all right; somewhere a balance is maintained.

Visits to the country can also lead to surprises. One day a man brought some delightful pieces of really top-grade jewellery to my hotel room. Every piece was good. The man was a fine-looking character, middle aged and very well-spoken. It broke my heart not to be able to buy that jewellery but I recognized many of the pieces. I had seen a lady wearing them when she visited my shop. A quiet twist of the conversation with the man brought me to the conclusion that the lady was his mother. When she had visited the shop I had admired them and asked if she would sell the jewellery. She smiled and shook her head.

'They are all I have left now,' she said. 'I sold so many nice pieces to help John when he was younger.'

I knew that she had a son called John but until he came to the hotel room, many miles away from the shop, I had not met him. I also knew that John had not contributed much to making life easy for his mother. A bad lot, but a charming one; never criminal enough to get on the wrong side of the law but bad enough to cause an upheaval in his family with his near misses at petty crime.

I told him to take the jewellery back to his mother, and if she wanted to sell it she would no doubt bring it to me herself. I think I was very savage that day. It was irritating not to buy the jewellery but pleasant to see the man's mother when she next came into the shop. She was wearing the jewellery.

'I asked John to get this jewellery cleaned for me,' she remarked rather petulantly.

Tactfully I found out that the date when she had asked dear John to do this coincided with the date when I was buying in her area.

'Never mind,' I replied cheerfully. 'They don't look too bad and I like to see you wearing the pretty things.'

She looked as pleased as indeed I felt!

I went on, 'If you want them cleaned; why not leave them with me whilst you do your shopping and I'll do it?'

At least I could try by these means not to let John get his fingers on the jewellery again.

She was grateful for the offer, and as I handed them back to her later on in the day I wondered what she would have said if she knew that the jewellery had been offered to me by her erring, but still beloved son? This was a time to let sleeping dogs lie. At least John would have to think up a very very good reason next time, before he got the jewellery in his possession.

I thought that was the end of the story until, a few months later, I picked up a newspaper and was horrified to read of the death of my customer. I felt even worse when, only a few days later, John came to the shop. He did not realize that I was the owner and I could see that he recognized me as the woman at the hotel fifty miles away. Although we did not mention that meeting we both remembered it.

I ended up with buying the jewellery, thinking that everything comes to the one who waits. I gave John less than a third of its real value and did not feel at all conscience-stricken about it. Deliberately I offered him a low price, knowing that whatever money he got for the jewellery it would not last him long and I might as well get the best of the bargain. I think at first I half hoped that he would refuse the offer, but he was too well mannered to haggle and the deal was quite painless. The jewellery meant nothing to him, he had not even taken the trouble to assess its value. All that mattered was that he would have a few pounds in his pocket. Well, he got just that and I despised him for it. Soon the jewellery was again sold.

On yet another trip to the country I was unwittingly drawn into the vortex of a family affair which turned out to be a positive brawl.

A beautiful elderly lady brought a magnificent, long string of pearls which she wanted to sell. The pearls were as handsome as their owner, ninety-four of them, and every one real. I found myself thinking that if I bought the pearls I would not have enough money to buy anything else, for I could not offer a chicken-feed price for them. This was the time to make a firm and quite a high offer. The lady also brought along her insurance policy for the pearls, and as I glanced at it I knew that my assumption of their value was very near the mark. Even allowing for a possible inflation of the price on the insurance, these pearls were going to cost a lot of hard cash.

I made my offer to the lady and she seemed quite satisfied with it, but said she would like a little time to think it over. She enquired when I was leaving and said she would 'phone me if she finally decided to sell. I waited in a tizzy all day for the 'phone to ring, I even had nightmares thinking that perhaps she would take them into the town and get other offers. I could not concentrate on anything. It seemed a happy omen that no one brought anything very good in to me, so the money for the pearls remained intact in my wallet. I badly wanted to spend the money, but only on those pearls.

Then at dinner that night the lady arrived with the pearls, which I was delighted to buy. I gave her my name and the address of the shop in the High Street, hoping that one day she might have more stuff to sell and would remember me. On my return to the shop I sold the pearls very quickly and profitably and dismissed them from my mind until a few weeks later, when a very blond, baby-faced man arrived in the shop. If ever I saw trouble brewing then it was on this man's face, and somehow the trouble was going to come my way. However, it was a bit early to jump to a wrong conclusion and the expression on his face may have been due to a bad breakfast. But in my heart I knew there was more to it than this. I approached him serenely enough with my usual 'Can I help you, sir?' but it was obvious that no one could help him much at all—and certainly not me. He was a blond bombshell of temper, just dying to explode right there on the spot. I waited for the explosion.

'You're the woman who bought the pearls?' It was lashed out from thin lips as an accusation, not a question.

I agreed that I was certainly 'the woman who had bought the pearls' but I could not see the point of his question at all.

'You bought ninety-four pearls three weeks ago; look, here is your receipt.'

He flung it at me as if it was a cheque that had bounced three times, yet I had paid for the pearls in fivers so there could not be any worry on account of the money being wrong. This was a time to think of Ahab and to walk delicately.

'Now, sir,' I replied, quite quietly, 'please tell me what the pearls have to do with you. I bought them from a lady——' He did not allow me to continue.

'Those pearls were mine.' He'd reached the screaming stage now. 'Do you hear me? *Mine!* And I want them back.' As he spat out every word as he advanced towards me, I began to pray that his bark was worse than his bite. I had to stand still for there was nowhere else to go in this small shop of mine. My goodness, he certainly could bark. . . .

'Now, sir . . .' I made it sound as near an insult as possible. 'You say I bought some pearls that belong to you and you have a receipt in your hand made out to another person. I can produce my proof of paying for the pearls; can you produce any proof of ownership?'

This reasonable request brought him to a standstill and he swallowed a few barks, almost choking in the process.

'Of course they are mine.' His tone was blustering.

'Well, you can hardly expect me to take your word for it.'

More swallowing of barks was making his face turn a puce colour.

'I am going to 'phone the lady from whom I bought the pearls,' and I made a dash for the 'phone.

Actually, I was dead worried. The first thought that struck me was that I had unknowingly bought some pearls that had been stolen. As I stood waiting for the 'phone number to ring I saw myself being carted away to the local magistrates' court. I felt small and pathetic until the voice at the other end of the line brought me back to earth.

I explained the situation to the lady from whom I had bought the pearls. She sounded very unhappy.

'It must be my son-in-law,' she said. 'I think I had better come right over. Suppose we meet and then I can explain everything.'

This seemed a good idea. Someone would have to do a good bit of explaining and the sooner the better as far as I was concerned.

The angry blond man seemed more upset than ever. When I suggested that he went for a walk and returned after lunch he started to argue, but finally went away with every show of a possible return in anger.

In due course the elderly lady arrived. Hardly had she wiped the dust of the road from her shoes when the bad-tempered son-in-law arrived as well. If he had been angry with me before he was now in an almost demented state. The sight of his mother-in-law was like the proverbial red rag to a bull.

Before I could say anything at all the pair of them had started a real slanging-match. To my surprise, my beautiful lady gave back as good as she got. I had visualized a quiet discussion between the three of us, but all I could do was to sit on the stairs waiting for a lull in the brawl before I could get a word in edgeways. Surely someone in the street would hear the commotion and call the police. No one did a thing. It needed just one member of the Noise Abatement Society to be passing the shop at that time to have had enough material to fill the correspondence columns of the newspapers for a week.

'Dear Sir,
    I was passing a shop in Ringwood when . . .' etc.

When the vases on the shelves began to perform a war-dance as a result of the vibrations set up by my two visitors I decided that I would have to join in the brawl myself. The air was blue with language that I hadn't heard since I left the Army.

I had to shout to make myself heard.

'Shut up!' I yelled—my voice was strident. The sudden shout of extra noise seemed to bring the other two down to a simmering point. We all retired to the foot of the stairs.

'Now, perhaps you would both be good enough to explain a few things to me,' I said firmly.

It all boiled down to the fact that the son-in-law considered that the pearls did indeed belong to him. More questions elucidated that the reason for this surmise was that the elderly lady had told her daughter that the pearls were left to her in her will. On finding herself without much money she decided to sell them, and, quite rightly in my opinion, had not seen fit to tell either her daughter or son-in-law about this decision. The son-in-law had found the receipt and saw himself being done out of his wife's inheritance. He must have had a very distorted process of reasoning, for I can think of no reason why the elderly lady could not change her mind about anything in her will. Obviously there had always been bad feeling between the lady and her son-in-law; today's affair would not be very helpful in deciding their future relationship.

I explained my point of view and showed them quite clearly

that I considered the whole affair to be in very bad taste. No one likes to be involved in family brawls. I had bought the pearls in good faith and paid a price that was agreeable to the seller, only to have my own shop made into a battlefield through no fault of mine. By now I was beginning to feel very bad tempered myself. I practically threw the pair of them out of the shop. Let them quarrel if they must, but not in my shop.

Mrs. Strong arrived back from lunch just as I was reaching the screaming stage myself, and as I was propelling my two undesirable customers into the street.

Dehydrated with past temper, they stood in the street looking the picture of crestfallen meekness. Mrs. Strong saw only the meekness, not realizing that it was sheer exhaustion after the battle that gave them such a pathetic look.

'I'm surprised at you,' said Mrs. Strong, in her most reproving contralto voice, 'losing your temper with customers. I thought you could be relied upon to keep calm.'

'Don't dare to lecture me,' I said, 'You don't know what I've gone through this morning with those two.'

I began to tell her, but the trouble with my manageress is that she always thinks I am exaggerating things. To her logical, ultra-sensible mind, it is inconceivable that 'nice people' should come into an antique shop and start bickering. They did it decently in the sacred precincts of their own homes.

She listened to all I had to say but I could see that I was going to be on a losing wicket for the rest of the day. I announced that I was going to retire to the flat over the shop in order to recover. As I went up the stairs I was muttering that I'd like to know what *she* would have done if it had happened when she was in the shop. Mrs. Strong has long ears; she heard every word of my mutterings. As I reached the top step she called to me.

'It wouldn't have happened at all if I'd been here,' she said sweetly.

Miserably, I don't believe it would.

'One day I'll give you such a piece of my mind,' I retaliated.

'Don't bother,' she said calmly. 'I know it, anyway.'

Basically, I suppose that is why we have got on so well during all these years.

I slammed the door of the flat, full of self-pity at being the most misunderstood woman who ever had the misfortune to have an antique shop in any High Street.

21
I'd have had it
if it had been a pair

I CAN visualize a situation in which a shoemaker has a shop containing nothing but left shoes! Imagine the shopkeeper having perhaps twenty or thirty customers each day, for five days a week, all admiring the left shoes, and, just as he thinks a sale is about to be completed, the fatal question, 'Oh, have you got the other one?' The average shopkeeper would be so frustrated and nerve-racked at the end of only one week that he would either give up the shop, shoot his first customer on Monady morning or commit suicide!

It says much for the sanity and balance of mind of the antique dealer that he can accept situations like this and take them in his stride. For every antique shop has some beautiful specimens of 'singles', a source of delight and hatred—delight in perhaps buying a Chelsea figure of rare craftsmanship, followed by hatred when the full realization hits you that no one will buy it unless you find the other one. Sometimes by a lucky coincidence with the cards stacked right for you and all the planets plus Lord Luck himself rooting hard for you, the elusive other half of a pair turns up. It *can* happen—but it has all the hazards of breaking the bank at Monte Carlo—perhaps once in a lifetime.

Since, these days, vases are not used very much for flowers, as the modern trend is to produce a little floral whimsy of a flower arrangement in a baby's shoe or suchlike fantastic article, there has arisen a use for all the odd vases which have accumu-lated on the shelves of any antique shop; for with the 'floral arrangement' fads there has also arisen another mania—that of making lamps out of strange objects. Fortunately vases are one of the favourite things for beginners, although price plays a more important part with the lamp-makers than with any other section of people. They have *always* got a sister who once bought a beautiful vase (just like *that* one—pointing to a single Cantonese vase) for only two shillings. Personally, I fear that some of my customers tell me great whopping lies at times! Not that it matters, but if there is one shop when the customer is *not* often right it is in an antique shop. Still, because of a vogue for home-made lamps with a different air, the odd vases now slowly disappear from the antique shops.

Perhaps the only really annoying customer who enters a shop like mine is the type who waits until you are offering a really nice pair of vases or carriage lamps. They come in and admire them greatly, and then say: 'But I want only *one*. Would you split this pair?'

At this time I play a little game, chiefly to hide the grinding of my teeth and the wicked words that I really want to say.

'Certainly, madam, we shall be pleased to split the pair, but you will understand that although the *pair* is twenty pounds we shall have to charge you seventeen pounds ten for one.'

This immediately causes a state of 'flux' in the mind of the prospective purchaser, for he sees you making the same price on the remaining vase or carriage lamp, and the thought hurts. Rumour has it that you make a fabulous fortune on every single piece of merchandise in your shop. *Now* they have proof of it. With infinite patience you must now disillusion them and gently but firmly 'give them the works'. Preferably stand between your customer and the only door, for it would be awful for them to escape before you have got all those wicked thoughts out of your head. Point out that you spend your life looking for *pairs* of things; that when you, personally, buy a pair you pay *extra* for this privilege. Therefore it is not logical to expect that if you are offering a pair of carriage lamps at twenty pounds you can sell one for ten pounds, and at some other date sell the remaining one for a further ten pounds. If you fall for this line of splitting pairs you will end up in a sorry mess, for possibly you have paid fifteen pounds for the carriage lamps. To sell one brings ten pounds back out of capital outlay, but you will be a long, long time with a debit of five pounds' outlay, even though you have one lamp left.

Since I have had a shop in the High Street I have never been able to discover where paradise is, but I do know that hell is the state that you discover in your own shop when you have numerous beautiful but, alas, single items languidly resting on your shelves. The amount of time and energy wasted in explaining to people that you have *not* got another one 'just like that' is the most wearying time that I ever experience.

There is also the awkward position of sometimes discovering that a pair is not a pair, and the hard truth that two of a like breed do not make a pair. I once bought two left-handed carriage lamps, magnificent ones too, and did not discover the fact until I was actually half-way through a sales talk on selling them! It became one of those hot-under-the-collar moments of awful embarrassment. Fortunately the day was saved by the fact that I had another pair in the shop, and by a rapid reduction of price I managed to transfer the affectionate attention of my customer to the lamps that really were a pair. It taught me a great lesson; now I try to check everything. Gold to me is never gold nowadays even if it is heavily stamped with a legible assay mark. It only becomes gold when it responds to the old acid test, and so with 'pairs'.

Another disturbing trend, which is insidiously beginning to disrupt the already tempestuous life of any antique dealer, is the sudden urge of the public to possess *pairs* of old garden urns. They are shockingly hard to obtain; even to *find* them is difficult. Having found them it is even more difficult to get the owners to part. The demand for *pairs* has never been higher, but amongst the many pairs I have bought this year I have also been tempted to buy many, many singles, chiefly because they have been of exceptional design. I can now see a vista of an Age of Urns unfolding in the future for me. In my lonely old age I shall stumble around my backyard in a wilderness of urns. So far I cannot think of any way of disposing of them, not even to the flower-arrangement fairies, and the Quaint Lamp Makers' Guild won't look at them! Possibly I shall have to make provision in my will for them, perhaps bequeathing them to distant relations or even to a few *bêtes noire*; certainly my single urns seem likely to be with me for the rest of my life. They stand in my patio, significant symbols of my bad judgment; graven reproaches for the mistakes I have made in buying them. But I am optimistic; somewhere in the world there may be someone who collects *odd* urns. If so, I beg him to contact me; I can add some interesting ones to his collection at very reasonable prices.

The trouble is that when you make a mistake with something the size of garden urns you cannot shut them away in a cupboard and pretend you never did it. They stand blatantly all over the place and have unhelpful habits. By virtue again of their size, where they are disgorged from the removal van there they must remain. Film producers may have a galaxy of stars, belted earls a covey of pheasants, but I—I have a *Reproach of Urns*; my own private mausoleum of mistakes and lost money. When the moon is shining, shadows and tricks of lighting make them appear twice as large and shadows give an appearance that they have increased in number, but always in odd ones. Over all, a chorus of ghouls sing in heavy dramatic chorus, 'I'd have had it if it had been a pair, been a pair, been a pair! . . .'

Cue for an antique dealer to shoot herself—oh yes, we have a funeral urn as well. You never know when *that* might be useful, do you?

22

From antiques to jazz
in several uneasy movements

THE usual conception of an antique shop is that it is something like a cross between a museum and a church. Indeed, I approach other antique shops with something like reverence myself, and there is always the temptation to speak in whispers. Unfortunately, my own shop has nothing of the austere feeling that makes my customers stupefied by its dignity and beauty. The shop itself is so small that to move anything is a major feat of engineering, and anything resembling a *trompe-l'oeil* type of display is absolutely impossible. I'd love to group Chinese ivories against a backcloth of rich velvet. I'd adore being able to put one exquisite rose in a single silver specimen vase. I've got the right ideas, but can never put them into practice. Space is valuable, and everything has to be crammed into the place. There are some days when I think that just one more item in it will cause the walls to give way. To date it has not happened. Even when I sell a lot of stock there never seems any appreciable difference in space. I live in a state of chaos with the only redeeming feature that I know exactly where everything is. When you live with chaos of your own making it becomes easy to remember where you have put anything, but I'd hate to work in anyone else's shop if it were like mine!

Years ago I resigned myself to being quite unable to put on a display that would make Bond Street jealous. Perhaps the reason why the customers like it so much is that they can potter and prowl around in the everlasting hope of digging out some treasure that I have half forgotten.

Even if I ever attained the gracious dignity of other shops I am quite certain it would not be maintained on one special weekend during the year.

It is a far cry from an antique shop to a Jazz Festival but on just one weekend in the year we are closely united. This is when the village of nearby Beaulieu is invaded by the 'Trad-fad-dads' and the 'beatnik beauties'. I think the fame of the Beaulieu Jazz Festival is known all over the world, but to feel its real beat you have to live within striking distance of it.

The invasion forces begin to take over in the area several days before the festival is scheduled to begin. The landscape is suddenly transformed into a living surrealist canvas whose characters grow before your very eyes. Long, thin, curly-haired, bewhiskered young men from Manchester; thin girls in black stockings and badly knitted, very long sweaters; short, rotund types with fresh, pink complexions from Wales. At the time of this year's festival, I was walking along the banks of the Avon when I met a very sad-faced young man dressed all in black. Instead of carrying the more usual uniform of the Avon bank settlers (i.e. a fishing-rod) he was carrying an enormous single mattress on his back. The mattress was not of the portable type for camping, but a robust hair-filled one. As he walked along he was playing a guitar! His feet were bare. Behind him there lumbered a pale-faced, red-haired girl in a bright-green jersey. She looked like a modern version of an Indian squaw following her brave to a new camping-ground. She lumbered because she was literally covered with camping equipment. A kettle and two mugs were tied round her waist; on her back a bulging haversack, and topping the haversack were two blankets. Wellingtons covered her feet and legs, and to help her on her way she was using a man's black umbrella.

I always believe in welcoming the strangers within our midst. Never let it be thought that we market-town folks are insular. I ventured a mild 'good evening' as we drew within speaking distance. The boy continued to play his guitar without answering; the girl didn't seem to have the strength left to muster more than the most feeble of smiles.

They were obviously a dedicated pair, but what worried me was that they were heading miles away from the road to Beaulieu. It was probably against some desperate principle to go direct to the Jazz Festival.

As time went on and we drew nearer to the weekend of the Jazz Festival, more and more strange sights were to be seen camping along the river-bank. The swans, with wisdom, disappeared to the upper reaches of the river. As the sound of transistor record-players and radios moaned through the air well into the night, I began to think I should have followed the swans and taken refuge on a small island towards Fordingbridge.

Our milk was missing from the step every morning during the invasion of the beatniks. I afterwards learnt that raiding parties moved into the High Street in the early hours quietly removing all bottles. I have got used to this as each year comes along and now take the precaution of fetching my milk direct from the dairy during beatnik week.

On the Friday before the Festival, after the shop was closed, the door-bell rang. I went downstairs to find ten assorted 'trad-dads' on the step. If you have ever opened the door to find ten trad-dads facing you, you will understand that it is quite an experience. My first thought was that they had been unable to find a camping site on the now well-filled river-bank and decided to take over the existing houses in the High Street. Ten Fidel Castros in assorted sizes at 8.30 on a summer's evening—it would make a stronger heart than mine begin to flutter.

The spokesman was pushed forward; I noted with relief that he was the smallest of the insurgents. If the worst came to pass I could battle with this one and slam the door, before the larger members of the contingent could go into action.

'Are you the second-hand woman?' he asked, quite quietly. I did a rapid recap and thought it would be safe to say that I was indeed the 'second-hand' woman. It had an odd sound about it, but this was an off-beat moment anyway.

'All right, boys,' said the spokesman, 'it's the right place.'

They swept me into the shop. The walls groaned a bit, but no danger was done to anything except me. The ten Castros were now firmly pressed round me.

'Is there anything you want?' I asked primly.

'Well, we heard you sold second-hand gear . . . like clothes. We want some really dandy gear.'

If there had been room for expansion I could have heaved a sigh of relief.

'You've come to the right place, boys; follow me.'

I led them down to my back room which is full of clothes of all ages and types. They swept on to the heaps of clothes like a crowd of hungry vultures on a corpse. In no time at all the tough Fidel Castros were dressed up into an even more exciting assortment of costumes than they had when they arrived. Bowler hats were fought over, tatty fur coats were grasped in eager hands. Army greatcoats and officers' jackets were held up for approbation.

Suddenly, I saw them all as small boys anxious to dress up, and before I could say 'trad-fad' I was joining in the game.

I took each one in turn and fitted him up in 'gear'. When we ran out of bowlers and fur coats we turned our attention to women's short, checked coats and sombreros. The transformation scene in Cinderella was nothing to the antics in my back room that night. To complete the picture, they all had walking-sticks or riding-crops. The conversation was a bewildering variety of modern jazz terms and schoolboy exclamations of pleasure. Each one paraded in front of the mirror and we had an impromptu mannequin parade complete with exaggerated stances which the model girls love.

Two hours and ten pounds later, they paraded out of the shop into the High Street, just as the public houses were turning out their customers. I stood on the step laughing and waving to them.

'We'll send you some more customers tomorrow, Ma,' one of the lesser Fidel Castros yelled.

'Disgusting,' snorted a well-respected resident of Ringwood, lurching home after a good session in the local.

I don't know whether I was pleased or annoyed when next day I discovered that they did indeed remember to send their friends. I arrived back from the bank to find Mrs. Strong surrounded by a screaming group of young beatniks. As it was a Saturday morning, and busy as well, I hustled them all into the back room, shut the door on them and left them to it. As each one queued up to leave the shop, I stood like a sergeant-major inspecting his recruits. I jotted down in a notebook what each beatnik was wearing and collected the money as each one left. A few haggled, but when I was firm and said 'It's this price or you take the clothes off', they paid up and laughed good-naturedly.

Mrs. Strong went off to lunch and said she hoped that things would be back to normal when she returned. She spent the whole afternoon making disapproving remarks about the invasion forces, many of whom were still parading up and down the High Street. By 5 p.m. the last of the trad-dads had left Ringwood for the Elysian fields of Beaulieu.

I went along to the Jazz Festival that night. My 'gang' had done themselves proud. I kept recognizing odd jackets as they flitted past me. The thing that amused me most was when I began to remember the different people from whom I had bought the clothes. I hoped that not too many of my Dress Agency clients were at the festival—they may not have seen it in quite the same light.

Unfortunately, as the years went, the Jazz enthusiasts deteriorated both in the taste in dress and their appreciation of the music. This year I felt a sigh of relief go through me when I heard that there would be no more festivals at Beaulieu. A colourful period in our local history has passed away, killed by the unruly conduct of a few hundred irresponsible hooligans. The Jazz Festival was a brilliant idea that went wrong somewhere along the line.

I shall never again sell any bowler hats and fur coats to ten Fidel Castros. It is an odd thought—or is it? Now that I come to consider the matter, it does not seem incongruous that trad-dads should come to my antique shop to seek out odd garments. After all, if they could dance on the lawns of one of the most glorious of Hampshire's stately homes, it doesn't sound as illogical as it seems at first thought. Jazz is really only antique music dressed up for a party.

23
Competition in the antiques game

ONE of the few trades that does not mind competition is that of antiques. Sometimes, when people look at a street where every alternate shop sells antiques, I know they wonder how anyone can make a living. It is not unusual to hear someone say,

'Goodness, I've never seen so many antique shops in such a small town!'

Ringwood certainly has its full quota of such shops, but no one to date has had to worry too much about competition. Actually, antique dealers are gregarious by nature and inclination. Any town that can boast of several antique shops will soon gain a reputation far afield. The advantage of this grouping system is that dealers coming from London will aim to spend a day and a night and possibly another morning in a town where there is more than one antique shop. It means that they can have several bites at the cherry. The dealers stand a chance of earning a day's wage in their travels by buying suitable goods from each shop to take back to their London depots.

However many antique shops there are in a town, there can never be two alike; many of them specialize in one type of goods as a backbone to their sales.

Ringwood has a good name amongst dealers, for they can come here on one beautiful buying-spree without wasting either time or petrol. I realize that it must be a surprise that the antique shops in Ringwood all do a thriving business. Even when a new shop opens, it does not cause any headaches amongst the existing shops of similar types. It becomes just another reason for putting Ringwood more securely on the map as far as the London dealers are concerned.

If you enter Ringwood from the Christchurch Road area, the first antique shop is a tiny but beautifully converted, sweetly pretty shop. It is aptly named 'the Matchbox'. It lurks discreetly near to the railway crossing and is owned by a retired army major and his enterprising little wife. They combine a love of antiques with being ardent members of the British Field Sports Association. If the shop is ever closed it is a safe bet that the owners are on an otter-hunting expedition!

Going over the level crossing, still keeping on the main road to the town, a visitor will come to the Bond Street type of shop which Ringwood can boast. Its enormous, double-bow-front windows are part of the architectural charm, guaranteed to make anyone stop and look twice even if they are not particularly interested in antiques. A large gate leads to a fine, spacious garden where anything from a gaily painted stage-coach, vintage car or iron Victorian garden seat is displayed. It is a shop to make any others look like poor relations, and it can have a most humbling effect on anyone like myself. It is a privilege and inspiration to look in the windows as I often do in the half twilight of a summer's evening. If I try to pass the shop on the other side of the road the bow windows bulge invitingly, to beg for examination at a closer point.

I have never been brave enough to go into the shop to enquire the price of anything, although I once saw a most charming goat cart which I would have dearly loved to own.

Only a few yards away from this gorgeous, well-stocked shop there is another bow-fronted antique shop. This time the windows are of Lilliputian size but they have all the attraction of anything miniature. The owner specializes in works of native character and the grotesqueness of some of the things displayed both fascinate and repel me. This shop started with one bow window when it was a cottage, then it gained another one when the owner bought the neighbouring cottage. With the added symmetry of double-frontedness a new dignity was added to this old part of Ringwood. Behind this shop there were once some delightful cottages with tiny flower-decked gardens. A delight for photographers, these cottages this year nearly caused many Ringwood residents to have apoplexy. A demolition order was about to be put into action when someone discovered that the cottages originally formed the meeting-place for the old Quaker community of Ringwood. A public meeting was held and controversy raged amongst councillors and residents alike. Local big-wiggery wanted to pull the cottages down, ratepayers wanted to retain them, but the men who pay the piper are not always entitled to call the tune.

Bureaucracy won the day and the bulldozers moved into the courtyard. In no time at all the old stone-and-mud walls came tumbling down, drowning the mutterings of the residents in a fine flurry of mechanical noise. Then a crack in the floor revealed that there was a vault-like chamber under the cottages and in the vault were *bodies*. The bulldozers withdrew and a new noise was created as reporters and journalists, amateur and professional photographers arrived to create a fine news story whilst the disturbed dust of centuries settled down again. Controversy flared up once more. The local archaeological society arrived armed with picks and shovels, after the police had removed the bodies. It became the fashion of the summer to devote every available moment to digging with commendable vigour, and honest sweat poured down some distinguished local faces. If you had paid your dues to the local society you could have the privilege of digging; if you were just a resident with a watching brief, well, you could just stand and watch. The 'Affair of the Bodies in the Vault' was more than a seven days' wonder, the news made the national Press and the television news service. After all, it is not every market town that can afford to demolish an early Quaker meeting-house. The buried bodies were removed with taste and discretion and probably given another burial. I know they were an encumbrance to the police and the local councillors. The former have work to do with the living and the latter were eager to get on with their plans to complete the demolition and make a car park on the spot for council refuse lorries.

Some people call this progress, others have another name for it, but I am sure that both councillors and residents could advance very good reasons for their views. For my part, I shall always remember the old Quaker cottages as being a most delightful corner of our market town. I used to cross the road to look at it, a simple little courtyard tucked away from the hectic, noisy traffic on the main road. Now it will be just another memory, and all too soon people will accept the fact that it is merely a car park for refuse lorries.

After the shop which once looked out on the picture-postcard cottages with their hollyhocks and roses round the door, there is a gap between our antique shops until Fridays' Cross is reached, where the main roads from Christchurch and Southampton intersect and the High Street begins. Scene of some of the finest traffic hold-ups in the south, Fridays' Cross now has the latest antique shop in the town, the 'Ringwood Galleries'. Perhaps it is cheating just a little because this shop so far specializes in high-class modern china and glass with just a sprinkling of antiques. But it is an imposing shop, well sited, splendid and clean with the gleam of new paint still on it.

Once there was a lovely art gallery and tiny antique shop on the Southampton Road but it is now an estate agent's office, the previous owner having decided to take his talent as painter and picture-restorer to some more appreciative and lucrative quarter.

From the 'Ringwood Galleries', the intrepid explorer in search of an antique shop must come down the High Street to my own shop. If he survives the shock the next stopping place is the Olde Cottage Tea Rooms. This is situated beyond the market-place on the banks of the River Avon. Ducks swim almost to the door, and here there is all the old-world charm that Americans would like to take back to their country but can't quite manage, even with money.

So they buy a souvenir and hope that some of the original charm will remain after a jet-propelled journey across the Atlantic. One day I must go to America to see our English antiques in their new American setting. It should be an interesting experience. By the time I can afford to go I expect many more of our national treasures, as well as our homely Ringwood ones, will have preceded me. Perhaps I may be lucky enough to buy an English antique in America as a souvenir of *my* journey. I know that many well-known dealers predict that many of the antiques in America will begin to flow back to England in the possibly near future. It seems a quaint but quite logical thought to me.

I must not forget a place that must surely be the most odd spot in Ringwood. Across the road from my own shop there is a tiny lane leading from the High Street to the car park, Meeting House Lane, again a reminder that once the Quaker sect had a stronghold in Ringwood. A few yards along the road a large, straight, bleak-looking building, two storeys high, juts out into the roadway. The place was once a stable but for several years now it has been a 'junk shop'. It is one of the most popular haunts for residents and tourists. The first impression that it gives is one of shock; if a building can have impact, then this building has it. The shop is open-fronted, its huge entrance, with goods spilling out almost into the road, presents an ever-open invitation to come in and look round. At times it gives the impression of something left over from a Christmas pantomime; a real-life Aladdin's cave within a stone's throw of the centre of the town, the sort of place that refuses to be ignored and it has the reputation of being able to supply everything from a spanner to the traditional white elephant or even a literal one.

The owner is a burly mountain of a man with a massive auburn beard. He views his domain with an air of gentle peacefulness. Not even the milling crowds who storm into the place during the summer can disturb his equanimity. This is one of the last strongholds of the old-type 'marine store'. If my own shop at times is chaotic, this store is doubly so. Lamps swing from the roof, pictures rest drunkenly on the walls, an antique chest is apt to stand cheek by jowl with an ex-army metal locker. The floor is covered with household goods, tools, garden figures, children's toys and mountains of books. Winter and summer the doors are wide open; the owner likes fresh air and appears to thrive in conditions that many another shopkeeper would despair about. People wander in and out at will, fascinated or appalled by the sheer amount of unusual articles in the store. In case the owner ever runs out of stock on the first floor, I can assure anyone that the second floor is also full from floor to ceiling. People buy and buy, and come back again to buy more. It has an insidious, haunting appeal to all types of people.

'I bet you don't know what you've got here,' a customer asks the man with the beard. He just smiles and assures them that hiders are finders. The owner doesn't in the least mind being known as 'the man who keeps the junk store'. I know that he has a business mind as large as his body and, being a North Country man, he also knows that 'where there's muck there's money'. I have known him to buy antiques with the same aplomb that he buys a thousand saucepans. It never strikes terror into his heart as it would do to mine. Whether it is saucepans, silver, old china or modern pottery he knows that there is a profit in anything bought at the right price and he doesn't despise making a shilling. 'There's only twenty shillings to the pound,' he says. 'Money soon mounts up, even in junk.'

I don't think that he has time for any special sales technique but he has an uncanny insight into the mind of his customers. Whatever they want, he is there to supply. He buys from sales, army depots, council houses and local mansions with the same easy-going manner that really hides his good business mind. Just as his sellers range over a large section of the community so do his customers. One minute he is buying riding-kit from a titled country family, another time he is buying toys from children. He is patient and kind with the children who haunt the place, particularly during the holiday periods, and considerate to elderly people. The bearded man has more patience than I could have.

Friendly rivalry exists between us. We are only a stone's throw away from each other and we frequently do a shuttle service between the two shops sending customers to each other.

There is a rumour in the town that if the 'junk store' or the shop in the High Street cannot supply what a person wants it is a miracle. So we work together on quite happy lines throughout the year. Sometimes I take time off to stroll across the road to see what my rival is displaying for the *pièce de résistance* of the day. I must admit that if I see anything that would look better in my own shop I go into a spirited haggle with the bearded one until I get the chosen piece for myself.

Really it is rather unfair to him, because the auburn-bearded owner of the local junk store is my husband! If you can't beat the opposition you may as well fraternize with it.

The policy has worked very well for more years than I care to count. Nothing is a better insurance for a happy married life than a mutual interest. It might be golf, riding or exploring. With us it is business. I am thankful that I married a man who has a rare kindliness of nature as well as a mutual interest in business.

Apart from the official antique shops in Ringwood, it seems to me that every other private house, at some time during the year, offers goods for sale to the public. It all begins in a simple manner, perhaps an object in one household is admired by a neighbour and a sale takes place.

All in the utmost good taste. Or perhaps an over-enthusiastic housewife, carried away by the excitement of a visit to the local saleroom, finds that she has bought a few things that simply do nothing to add to the attraction of her own home. The obvious thing to do is to sell. This selling business becomes a disease, and is liable to get a person in its snares. Before the housewife knows what she is doing, she is carried away by the heady feeling that a profitable sale can give. Next time she goes to a sale she remembers that she could have sold a pair of surplus vases to three different people. So she buys another pair of vases and with luck sells them.

The High Street in Ringwood is plastered with little post-card notices in shop windows offering goods for sale, and these include everything from prams to antiques. I know practically all the people who display cards regularly, and for the modest outlay of about ninepence they have a good cheap advertising medium, which I know always brings results. I have also noticed that many cards, dutifully changed weekly, offer articles for sale throughout the whole fifty-two weeks of the year. Pin-money for the housewife? Maybe it is, but it seems to me that in many cases a safe profitable business is being carried on from many discreet hearths in the town. The charm of this type of business is that it is free from income tax. There is nothing to prevent any-one from selling 'surplus goods' and who is to say if they are indeed surplus from a private house or articles bought purely with the intention to sell again? Shopkeepers can be undercut in price by sellers from private houses, who have no startling over-heads to consider.

It is money for old rope really and a much better prospect than going out to work, and there is no restriction on age groups by this 'card-in-the-window' form of salesmanship.

I always enjoy doing some shop-window reading when I walk down our High Street; it can be quite fascinating. As I know nearly every house and occupant in the area, the cards can also contain some elements of surprise to me.

'Pram for sale, fair condition, reasonable. Apply before 6 p.m.' The address follows.

I know that the woman at this address has six young children, which probably accounts for the 'fair condition' of the pram. I also remember that she is about thirty-five years old. The thought strikes me that she may not be wise to sell this pram. Or maybe she is just ambitious to get a spanking brand-new pram. I also remember that her husband returns home at 6 p.m. and even with the best of husbands it is perhaps desirable not to let them know everything. Let him remain in ignorance of the extra little perks which boost the morale of the housewife and increase her pay-roll.

Well, well, *well*! I never expected to see that address on a sales card in a shop window! I recognize the description of a plated silver tea-service as one which I sold from my own shop some months ago. Lovingly I remember the haggle we had to induce the sale and I note with approval that the person now offering it for sale has cleverly added seven pounds ten shillings to the original purchase price. Mentally I wish her luck in the sale; if she brings it off she is a better saleswoman than I am. The tea-service was a bargain when she bought it from me and would stand about three pounds being added to the price. But seven pounds ten is stretching it a bit too far even for the most brilliant of saleswomen. It is nice to be able to take a personal interest in things that have once been for sale in my own shop. I take my hat off to the clever bargain-hunting housewives of the town.

Who can dare to say that the lot of the country woman in a market town is ever dull? I will agree that everyone is a shop-keeper at heart, but a dull life—never!

Think of the interesting chats that can be had over a pleasant cup of tea by their own fireside whilst selling a piece of furniture to a visitor. It is all so ultra-respectable. No regular hours to keep and life need not be organized by the opening-and-shutting, day-by-day routine of a shop. No standing in draughts whilst a customer makes up her mind, no queuing to wait one's turn to be served. Multiply each card seen in a shop window by a potential three customers and the total can be a staggering amount of business done quietly and unobtrusively in the discreet precincts of a private house.

24
Call me Aunty

IT WAS one of those utterly sordid days when trade was so slow that Carey Street seemed to be only just around the corner. The few customers who came into the shop were an unhappy bunch, seeking only to sell dismal pairs of vases of uncertain age and no character. Also it was Friday the thirteenth! It came as no surprise to me therefore when my manageress chose the day to inform me yet again that she would 'have to go'. We had a little spitting-session before I arrived at the conclusion that I would be better out of the shop for the rest of the day. I mentally washed my hands of my staff and customers, leaving Mrs. Strong to vent her spleen on the copper and brass. By tomorrow I was sure that everything would be all right; she really likes her job—is very good at it, and I appreciate her work and generally sensible outlook on life. Still, we have to have our little scream at each other periodically. I find when this happens that if I mutter darkly about banishing her to the dim realms of our Press Agency (second-hand clothes shop to the uninitiated!) that matters begin to calm down. On the other hand, Mrs. Strong can retaliate by reminding me of her past happy days when she was receptionist to a most respectable dentist and was very happy. She follows this up with references that she's heard 'that the optician next door needs an assistant, only half the hours and twice the money'. At this point I bang the door, mutter frightful words in any language that seems appropriate, knowing that she will retaliate in an English that resolves into delightful pure cockney!

Anyway, it was *this* type of day when I went upstairs in search of peace and quietness. I was moodily stoking up the sitting-room fire with sawn-off logs of wormy old furniture, and playing a lovely old record of Menuhin performing a Mozart Adagio which seemed to fit the mood of the day. The fire was just beginning to blaze nicely at the much-varnished wood when up the stairs stumped my old friend Cecil.

'Ah-ha,' he said. 'Business can't be as bad as *that*.' He was looking meaningly at the shambles of half-chopped-up furniture and in his nice gentlemanly way implying that I was burning the furniture because I couldn't afford any coal. His obbligato of 'Your tiny hand is frozen' did nothing but ruin the Mozart, so I turned the record off and decided to string him along.

'Yes,' I said, 'business is so bad. I'm burning the tables next and after that I'll start on the doors.'

Cecil wound himself into a chair; being very tall and very, very thin, this was quite a performance. He obviously intended to stay and maliciously I marked down his chair as the next one for burning.

'Tell me all about it; have you been reduced to a paltry ten per cent profit today? Too bad!'

'Well, I've got a final demand for Income Tax, and notice to quit the storehouse from one of my landlords. The police have been investigating a jewellery theft and want to know if I've bought the stuff, the dog's eaten my dinner and Mrs. Strong's given me her notice. . . . How's that for a start?'

He gave horrible wheezing crackling sounds which indicated laughter.

'What you need is a change. Let's go out to dinner.'

Sourly I asked him if it is a firm invitation, or do I pay half? By now I am very suspicious. If *he* invites me out to dinner he wants to know something! After he assured me that it was indeed a firm invitation, I told him to name the time and the place, thinking all the while that whatever it was he wanted to know, he needed to know quickly. 'Seriously,' said Cecil, 'you do need a change. You sit here every night looking at your old stamp collection, and you aren't getting any younger.'

I stared balefully at him, reminding myself that he'd seen far more birthdays already than I had. The day drifted uneventfully into the evening and I got myself ready to go out. Putting on my glad rags to paint the town red for me resolved itself into putting on my best rings and ear-rings, two forms of adornment which I prefer to any type of rustic Dior model clothes.

We met at seven and went to the local hotel, where we had a very pleasant meal. When we reached the mixed-grill period I learnt that Cecil wanted to know something about a picture which he knew was in a house to which I had often been invited as a friend. Not even a bottle of wine had mellowed me sufficiently to impart any of the things I had observed about the picture on my frequent visits to the house. I could feel Cecil rapidly losing his appetite. Just when I was about to relent at the Grand Marnier and coffee stage, we were joined by two other people, whom I knew by sight but not by name.

'My dear Cecil,' said the lady. 'How nice to see you again, and Mrs. Leek too. We're giving a dinner party tomorrow, won't you both come?'

Cecil is truly magnificent at times like this; local society loves him and he is always being invited out to cocktail and dinner parties. To my horror he accepted the invitation on behalf of both of us. His friends went out of the dining-room as I glared at him.

'What on earth did you do that for? You know I never go out to dinner parties in private houses.'

'Do you good,' he said pleasantly. 'Do you a world of good to get out a bit and mix with people away from the business. Trouble with you is that you have no social life at all; you're that frightful thing, a woman in business.' He shuddered so much the waitress thought there was something wrong with the coffee.

By the time I went home I was almost convinced that he was right. It might be a good idea to go out to dinner and forget the business. By the next evening I was actually looking forward to the dinner party and we went off by taxi to arrive at a quite over-poweringly lovely house on the outskirts of the town.

As we went in I recognized a few pieces of furniture which

had formerly graced my shop, and as a result I began to feel more and more comfortable. There seemed to be a large number of people about, but it was a gracious, spacious house. I recognized a lot of people that I knew as clients. Cecil disappeared to greet other old friends of his and I found myself eying the furniture and silver almost analytically. Even when I was joined by a doctor who treated my children for various childish ailments I couldn't stop working out the market price of the silver. It had just reached a nicely rounded four-figure sum when I became aware of a very sweet girl trying to attract my attention. In the middle of a soliloquy on the virtues of diphtheria inoculation I excused myself to the doctor and joined the girl.

'I say, Mrs. Leek,' she said softly. 'Will you be in the shop tomorrow?'

I assured her that I most certainly should be in the shop on the following day, that as it was Wednesday and market-day, I should more or less be chained to the floor from 9 till 6 p.m. She seemed awfully relieved at this simple remark and went on: 'Then I'll call on you at about eleven. Will you be alone?'

In a flash it dawned on me that this dear sweet young thing would probably call on me to sell me something; the party spirit in me began to die a slow death as I assured her gravely that I would be quite alone.

'Oh, good,' said the young creature, moving very close to me and murmuring, with a conspiratorial air, 'And you won't tell my husband about *anything*, will you?'

By now I was quite worried. All I'd done was to be persuaded by Cecil to come to a simple dinner party to get away from business, only to find myself about to be dragged into someone's domestic affairs where a sweet young wife doesn't want her husband to know that she is going to visit me. Desperately I looked for Cecil, but he was engaged in an animated conversation with our hostess and deliberately ignored me.

At dinner I sat next to a solicitor and before I could say 'see you in court' he was off at a gallop on a matter of valuation for a client of his. He was so intense and professional and I got so carried away with it myself, that I forgot to continue eating the asparagus and someone removed it, thinking I didn't like it. This annoyed me very much as it is one of my favourite dishes. Instead of enjoying it, all I'd done was to land myself with a date at the solicitor's within the next two days.

Coffee was served in the lounge and my hostess was kind enough to take me on one side and invite me to look at her latest picture which she hoped would prove an investment as well as an aesthetic pleasure. The party took on a dismal aspect as I looked at the picture, knowing that my hostess liked it and that I didn't. It is doubtless expensive, but of the type that anyone can buy on the South Coast of France by the hundred, if brave enough. It made me quite unhappy and I realized only too well my own social inability to express even a modicum of pleasure. Fortunately I was saved by the appearance of Cecil who beamed on his hostess, saying kindly but firmly, 'My dear Moira, you always had the most curious taste in pictures.' I knew he hated the picture as much as I did but he has a wonderfully tactful way which I'll never have as long as I live. Our hostess glided away to join her other guests leaving me alone with Cecil.

'So . . . oooo,' I hissed at him. 'You bring me here to get away from it all? Do you realize I've got a mysterious assignment with a sweet young thing who probably wants to pop her husband's latest anniversary present, a date with a solicitor to view some silver and I nearly told our nice hostess *exactly* what I thought of her picture?'

He roared with laughter. 'Don't worry, the night's still young, time for loads of fun yet. Have a good time; this'll make a new woman of you. Ha, here comes Mrs. Bromsky, you'll like her; member of the local Dramatic Society.'

Mrs. Bromsky approached, an intense, well-preserved, middle-aged lady, who I knew had once been an actress. Already I could see that she had the presence. She made a wonderful entrance, sweeping down on me, hand beautifully extended at just the right angle. I felt almost like curtseying.

'Oh, dear Mrs. Leek.' The diction was superb. 'This will

save my calling on you tomorrow.' (Hurrah for something, I breathed.) 'We're doing *Gigi* next week at the cinema, could you help us with some of the furnishing effects?'

How could I say no? She was so absolutely regal. I found myself involved in another date when she would call to discuss 'props' with me. Just a chandelier, a French settee, a nice little commode—oh, and a few really choice bits of French porcelain will be all that she required. Weakly I murmured acquiesence. She was so enthusiastically grateful that I was sure that I was a mean old thing not to be more gracious myself. As she glided away to a perfect exeunt she paused for a final word.

'And, of course, you won't forget the straw hat and striped dress for darling Gigi, will you?'

I decided to be swept away with the whole thing. Wildly I promised to furnish the set and dress the whole show, right down to the carnation in Ton-Ton's buttonhole.

So this was a party! As I sank tiredly into an easy chair I found I was twice as exhausted as I feel after a tough market-day in the shop, and Cecil had said the night was still young! As I drooped tiredly into the chair I could hear a murmur of voices. 'Of course, you know who *she* is?' said an unknown voice. 'She has that shop in the High Street; you can sell anything there. No, the shop hasn't got three brass balls outside but everyone calls her Aunty. I believe her real name is *Leek*.' The voice dissolved into well-bred masculine laughter.

I gathered that I was the cause of this and the idea amused me too. So I'm called 'Aunty', am I? Well, many places have pawnshops and their various 'Uncles', but Ringwood is different, it has Mrs. Leek as an 'Aunty'.

Cecil arrived to enquire why I was squirming with laughter. When I repeated the overheard conversation to him he was quite surprised that it was news to me that the local boys call me 'Aunty'. That man knows everything! The evening drifted on quite pleasantly and we took our leave assuring our hostess that it had been quite, quite delightful. On the way home Cecil appeared to be a man with something on his mind, and I was very suspicious. He hadn't been drinking very much, he'd had a good time and, as always, he'd been a huge success with the ladies. What then, was brewing?

There was only one thing, blunderbuss tactics!

'Come on, tell me the worst?'

'Well,' he said. 'We-ll, I've invited a few people along tomorrow night for a party.'

'So what? And *who* have you invited?'

He reeled off a list of people so long that I gave up counting them after the first three dozen.

'And where are you going to dine and wine a cup-tie crowd like that?'

'Well.' He hummed and ha'd and well'd so that I knew there really was something bad on that bright mind of his. I also knew that somehow I was implicated in something that I was not yet fully aware of. There are few occasions when Cecil is at a loss for words. A terrifying half-formed idea struck me as I did a swift recap of the limitations of Cecil's home. He encases his quart-sized body every night into a pint-sized cottage in which a dinner party of anything like the size he had outlined was obviously a sheer physical impossibility. I insisted upon knowing more about it.

'Come on, give!'

He too decided on blunderbuss tactics.

'I thought, as you have such lovely big rooms, we'd hold the party at your place.'

I was completely stupefied, then the full realization of his words hit me like a bullet. I screamed as if I'd been hit; so effective was the scream that the taxi-driver looked backwards, slowing down to assure himself that all was well in the back of his vehicle.

'*You!*' Of all the rank cheek, this exceeded everything!

'It'll be all right.' He tried to be soothing, contrite and wheedling all in one effort. 'I'll get all the food and drinks organized, you just get some flowers and a few clean tablecloths; it'll be all right, really.'

'Do you realize that tomorrow I'm burning the tables? And the doors? A fine party that will be. Why don't you try sitting at home one night and read a good book instead of throwing out party invitations willy-nilly—at my house, indeed!'

'Don't worry so,' he said. 'They'll love it; we'll have a buffet instead of a sit-down do, then you can burn the tables if you want to.' A concession indeed!

'Oh, all right.' I sounded as ungracious as I felt. 'But don't blame me if they never speak to you again.'

As I entered my large flat I couldn't quite see Cecil's friends tripping gracefully around on my big threadbare carpet. The rain came through the roof one day and did shocking things to the ceiling, and no amount of builders and decorators have been able to stop big fungus-like growths suddenly appearing on the ceiling in the top corner of the lounge. I toyed with the idea of not removing them before the party, although I perished the thoughts of tampering with the drinks, or serving nothing but the foulest of Red Biddy.

'After all,' said Cecil airily, 'it's time you had a house-warming here, do you good——'

'To get away from business.' I finished it for him. 'Just remember though that this will probably be the end of a beautiful friendship, and I'm not responsible for anything that may happen.' I put a fine lot of venom in this sentence but he was oblivious to it. He was getting brighter every moment as he said: 'I know. You invite a few people too, then you can call it a house-warming.'

This cheered me up immensely as I decided to invite my old friend Domenic. Nothing like mixing the guests. I liked the idea, for Domenic was a character to end all characters. A Romany— the idea intrigued me so much that I was in danger of becoming enthusiastic myself.

'All right, don't forget to order the food.'

He left, blissfully happy.

Next day I told Mrs. Strong that we were going to have a party.

'What, here?' She was quite unbelieving. 'Who's coming?'

As I reeled off the list of guests she was suitably impressed, for she knew nearly every one of them. All day long we had a constant stream of errand boys running up and down the stairs with boxes of all shapes and sizes. I had to fight my way into the kitchen, and at once I was stricken with horror. *All* this food couldn't be consumed in one night, surely? The man had gone mad and invited them for a week at least! I rang Cecil to verify this and was most relieved to hear that it was indeed to be only a one-night party. I didn't forget to mention that I'd paid out numerous small sums to sundry errand boys as tips and that the amount would make his petty-cash account look mighty sick. He was too elated to worry and arrived at five o'clock ready to 'help'. But by now Mrs. Strong had the entire staff of the various Leek shops completely organized and he was allowed only to grill the sausages. Miraculously, the flat appeared to take on a festive air and I felt mean that I had ignored the fungi. It was too late then to attempt to remove it, and I could only pray that the guests would either ignore it or regard it as an original form of modern décor.

About half the entire population of Ringwood seemed to be assembling when there was a shattering peal on the door-bell of the shop. Mrs. Strong volunteered to answer it, returning quickly to speak to me in frantic sign-language that she urgently needed me. I manœuvred my way to the top of the stairs.

'It's Domenic,' she said. 'What shall I do with him? He's got a lamp in his hand, but he never comes at this time of night. I didn't know what to say.'

I had forgotten to tell her that Domenic was invited to the party; I hardly expected him to come, as he can be an elusive character and liable to steer clear of any form of humanity when the mood takes him. I went down to the shop to find Domenic looking like a miniature Haile Selassie. Tonight he had excelled himself. After we had done a delightful haggle over the lamp resulting in neither of us losing any face at all we went upstairs. Domenic made a world-beating entrance. He was resplendent in traditional Romany costume; long-waisted black moleskin coat, drainpipe trousers and a gay Romany neckerchief. To complete the picture he wore his best gold ear-rings and three gold rings on the fingers of one hand and a big, impressive gold sovereign on the other. The original Haile Selassie couldn't have made a bigger impression if he had arrived in person.

'Don't introduce me to anyone,' said Domenic, eying the crowd mournfully. 'I'll sort this lot out for myself!'

Needless to say he was a tremendous success and everyone stopped admiring the fungi on the ceiling to take in a good eye-ful of Domenic. Even Cecil was slightly shaken by the appearance of my special, black-haired, bearded friend with his air of decayed Edwardian splendour.

The party appeared to be going with a swing, especially when Domenic softened up sufficiently to give a wonderful exhibition of his prowess in being able to imitate every known dialect in England as he began to tell his stories. I found people were calling me darling, while Mrs. Strong summed everything up as 'a right Chelsea mob in there'. I noted that she seemed to be enjoying herself.

I became overcome with the happy glow that any hostess finds as she realizes that her party is definitely a success. Even the orange tones of the fungi didn't seem out of place, and I am now convinced that there is a great future in orange fungi as a new means of décor. After all, more outrageous things have already become a success!

Cecil was doing shocking things with bottles of liquid, pouring them into a huge punchbowl and wildly filling everyone's glass with the brew. Whatever he put in it, must have been potent, because I noticed many of the guests were becoming glassy-eyed.

'You'd better stop that,' I said as he grated lemon peel with great violence into the bowl. 'What'll we do if this lot passes clean out on our hands?'

'Don't worry, gal,' he said. 'This crowd trains daily on neat gin and whisky; they've got cast-iron stomachs.'

Before we knew where we were it was 4 a.m. and a new

day was dawning. We all squeezed into the kitchen and began to fry bacon-and-eggs. My God! They *had* got iron stomachs!

As a grey thin dawn crept down the High Street our guests began to disappear, and suddenly it was strange to find the house quiet, with mountains of empty glasses and entrée dishes, with cigarette-ends and cigar-butts carousing in receptacles never meant for them, and, to my amazement, there wasn't a scrap of food to be seen anywhere! Only Domenic, Cecil and I were left. Cecil eyed the dirty dishes balefully and disappeared to his pint-sized cottage before he could be involved in any washing up. I went down with Domenic to his car in the side lane by the shop. After listening to gurgling noises we came to the conclusion that it was too early in the morning for it to consider doing any work. In short, the car wouldn't budge. We shoved, pulled, kicked and cursed; we wiggled knobs and encouraged it in every known way, but it beat us. Domenic took it all very philosophically.

'That's that,' he said. 'Don't worry, I'll sleep in the garden.' Knowing that it was no use at all to offer Domenic a bed in the house, I waited while he squeezed himself into the garden between the urns and marble figures. He curled up like a cat, oblivious of the chilly morning air, tilted his black velour trilby over his face and in half a moment he was fast asleep.

I didn't feel at all worried about him and went to my own bed.

Next morning, amongst a hundred other bells ringing in my head, I discerned one which was undoubtedly that of the telephone. I staggered towards the 'phone but someone had made the floors slope even more than usual. There was an impression of the ceiling being pressed down on my head whilst brutal little men were holding on to my eyelids. Someone must have pole-axed me whilst I slept, only this could account for the terrible way I felt. The 'phone rang relentlessly, and despite the sloping floors I managed to reach it.

It turned out to be an elderly neighbour who lives in a cottage in the side lane. She sounded worried; her voice fluttered with it, making my ears tingle with the vibrations.

'*Mrs. Leek*,' she said, and even in my present state I could feel that she was aghast about something very vital; the words came through in capital letters. 'Mrs. Leek, are you aware that there is a most strange man in your garden? I think he is asleep—or *dead*.'

For my part I was beyond caring even if the garden was strewn with corpses but I was forced to make some answer to the excited voice at the other end of the 'phone.

'Oh yes, Mrs. Bowyer, just one moment, I'll look through the window.' I couldn't see through the window though so I made the fatal mistake of opening it. . . . I should have known better! The morning air with all its health-giving qualities struck me straight between the eyes. In a swirling mistiness I looked down to the garden and saw Domenic, sleeping as peacefully as a baby, doing no harm to anyone. What on earth was the woman making so much fuss about!

The fresh air treatment although violent at first, seemed to bring me back into the world, and I could answer the 'phone.

'You're perfectly right, Mrs. Bowyer, there *is* a man asleep in my garden.' I felt that the occasion demanded great solemnity. 'Don't worry, I expect he'll wake up soon. Goooooood-bbye. . . .'

The voice at the receiving end of the 'phone began to get more excited and rose in tonal quality to almost a raucous state, the only thing to do was to replace the receiver, very, very gently.

'Cooo,' I muttered to myself. 'I'll kill Cecil when I see him. Damn him and his party.'

It was a good thing I didn't see him until much later in the day; as a matter of fact I didn't actually see very much at all that day. He arrived in the late afternoon just as we were closing the shop. Without any preliminary chatter he began.

'Now, about *tonight* . . .'

'Nothing at all about tonight,' I said icily. 'We've painted this town red enough for one week. I'm a wreck and I intend to have a quiet evening at home, *alone*. Oh yes, it may seem dull to you, but at heart I'm just a simple country wench who needs peace and quietness, for ever.'

He refused to take the hint and I decided it might be easier to let him talk rather than argue with him.

'We promised Mrs. Bromsky we'd go to the dress rehearsal of Gigi.'

'Did we now?' I was belligerent.

'We must go, she'll be frightfully offended if we don't.' The thought of offending the regal Mrs. Bromsky, whom I now rated as practically on the same status as royalty was too much for me. Ah well, I sighed, we may as well end the week as we began, then start afresh next week.

'All right,' I agreed. 'Gigi it is!'

We went down to the Community Centre where the dress rehearsal of Gigi was to be held. Fortunately it is not very far from the shop. As we went into the hall we were met by another lady who greeted Cecil very cheerfully.

'Hello, Mr. Alexander, here you are with Mrs. Leek again.'

I didn't like the way she said 'again'. I could foresee the local grapevine twittering its roots up with the news that Mr. Alexander had been out with that Mrs. Leek every night last week.

Ah well, some call me Aunty and some call me other things. It's all part of the fun in the High Street.

The stripes on Gigi's dress started to play havoc with my tired old eyes.

It had been a week and a half; back to the stamp collection on Monday. I agreed with Cecil, though. It *was* a good party!

25
Pornography in porcelain

UNTIL I owned an antique shop I had a certain naive innocence about many things, including pornography. I always associated it with the written word and of course as a sordid relation of the art of photography. I suppose the average person never thinks seriously about pornography, except when the subject is brought up in the columns of a newspaper. Yet when it enters suddenly into a person's life, as it did in my own, there is always an element of shock. Unless, of course, you are the sort of person who goes around looking for pornographic subjects. In normal circles the subject is often regarded as a joke, everyone at some time or other has heard snickering 'funny' stories connected with 'you buy dirty postcards, yes?' type of thing.

My own introduction to pornography came as a startling fact that it is the subject for very big business. The shock part came when I actually met, or heard of, the people who buy dirty postcards with the seriousness of connoisseurs; the people who look for pornography, who actually want to buy it, and who ultimately, I suppose, get a strange vicarious pleasure from it.

My first active realization of pornography came about because of a very innocent adventure in buying a desk. I have always had a craze for wanting to buy desks; they are my favourite type of furniture. One day I was in the country and bought a desk from a lady. She told me that it had belonged to her deceased husband who had been a schoolteacher at the local village school. The desk was large and beautifully made. I bought it, and when I got it back to the shop I went into the usual routine of trying to find out if it had a secret compartment. The Victorians loved to indulge in whims of carpentry whereby a secret recess could be skilfully hidden. They often made it extremely difficult to find, and searching for it is a fascinating part of buying a desk. This particular desk, I felt sure, must have a secret compartment. I tried all the usual tricks, pressing numerous knobs that did not seem to have any other reason for being there than to disguise some secret place. I took the tiny drawers out from the inside of the desk, measured the overall width against the width from the back of drawers to the front ledge. There was a three-inch gap in the comparison of the measurements. This desk simply *had to have a secret compartment.*

Mrs. Strong and I spent every available moment delicately trying to find it, but it was weeks after we had almost given up all hope that it revealed itself. I don't think we were very concerned that we should find anything of interest in the compartment beyond an odd love-letter. Our main interest had been to find the trick part of the desk; we hated to be defeated.

So when I put my hand into the compartment and found it packed tightly with cards I was pleased. Mrs. Strong joined me as I drew out a handful. She gave them one look and retired from the desk as if she had been shot. Every card in my hand was a pornographic postcard of the most lurid type! We cleared everything out of the recess to find that we were now the possessors of some five hundred postcards. All of the same doubtful character, guaranteed to raise a blush on even our age-hardened faces.

Many of the cards were printed in Germany but a few were produced in London. Most of these were of the glossy photo type and must have been very expensive to produce.

Legally, I suppose, they belonged to the woman from whom I had bought the desk but I could hardly send them back to her. We knew her husband had had the reputation of being a most respected member of his profession. The whole thing made me sick, when I thought of the man who collected stuff like this and at the same time had children in his charge. It set up a whole panorama of horrible thoughts. We burnt the cards discreetly in our lounge fire late at night. I suppose there must have been over a hundred pounds' worth of money going up in smoke that night. It gave me a peculiar feeling to be burning what I knew must be a good potential cash profit, but it had to be done.

To trade in pornography is dangerous, and as bad as being a buyer of it. I did not feel clean until the last card had been burnt and I always looked at the desk with resentment. Worse still, I was actually glad that the owner of the desk was dead; at least he would not be teaching any more children.

Naturally, after a time, Mrs. Strong and I had many laughs over the affair. Whenever we had a customer in asking for post-cards (legitimate ones, that is) we had this secret joke between us, wondering what the customer would have said if we remarked:

'Sorry, sir, no postcards today; only five hundred porno-graphic photos. . . .'

From that date I always viewed any innocent albums of photos and postcards with something like alarm. If an innocent desk can yield a crop of pornography it is as well to be prepared against a further shock to the system.

My next introduction to pornography was not quite so startling, and at least I did not have the sheer weight of numbers to contend with.

I bought a collection of Chinese porcelain from a private house which included a most beautiful pair of enamelled figures. They were mounted on a carved hardwood stand in the usual way of Chinese porcelain. The workmanship was magnificent and the enamelling extremely fine. When Mrs. Strong looked at the faces of the figures she surprised me by saying she thought they had a leery look about them, although many Chinese figures have this peculiar grotesque appearance which adds to their interest and charm to the collector. The annoying thing about the porcelain figures was that they had been glued to the hardwood stand. In a moment of enthusiasm for work I decided to release the figures from the stand in order to clean both parts. Carefully I prised the porcelain away from the stand, without doing any damage to either. Then I looked at the underneath part of the figures. All I can say is that the same meticulous workmanship and colouring, so apparent on the upper part of the figures, was carried out with wonderful craftsmanship and in detail. I think it was the accent on the 'details' that was so shocking; nothing was missing or left to imagination. Pornography in porcelain was something I had never dreamt of seeing. True, the makers of Staffordshire figures at times did crude things with their funny little figurines such as 'last to bed turns out the light'. This was something quite different —repulsive, but it did not have the same effect on me as the postcards.

Well, you can burn pornographic postcards but it is more of a problem to dispose of anything in porcelain. I simply could not bring myself to destroy the figures. When they were standing on the hardwood plinth they looked so beautiful, and innocent enough to grace anyone's china cabinet.

I began to understand that leery look, though.

We Sellotaped the figures securely on to the stand and tucked them away at the back of the shop where they attracted a lot of attention. We told people that we did not want the figures handled. One day a very sweet, elderly lady came into the shop. She looked exactly like any vicar's sister and probably was. She spotted the figure and began to purr over it.

'My sister had a Chinese figure just like that,' she said.

Truly I hoped that her sister was not 'that type of woman', and I made every effort to divert her attention to other pieces of Chinese pottery. She was an obstinate type, though. The more I tried to attract her attention, the more she harped back to the Chinese figures. She raved about the craftsmanship, she admired the enamel and she handled them as if she had fallen in love with them.

'How much are they?' she asked. 'They would look so nice with the one my sister has.'

'Twenty-five pounds,' I said, hoping that the price would knock her for a boundary. To my surprise it bounded off her like a feather. It was an odd feeling not to want to sell something to a customer. As Mrs. Strong passed me she gave me a gentle nudge; her nudges are always discreet so the customer does not notice. I gathered that Mrs. Strong wanted me to notice what the lady was doing.

I was stricken to see that her long nervous fingers were quietly peeling off the Sellotape. Quietly but firmly I leaned forward and took the figures from her, placing them high up on a shelf over her head.

'I am awfully sorry,' I said, 'but my assistant has just told me that we have already given a customer the option on these particular pieces.'

She looked a bit annoyed but I began to coax back her interest in a very nice Chinese pot with a kylin on the top. If I had to knock this piece down to rock-bottom price I would be prepared to sell it to her—anything to keep her happy and her attention away from the figure.

Mrs. Strong added charm and a load of sales talk to my own, and finally we sold her the porcelain pot.

I wrapped it up with relief.

Next day I went to a sale, leaving Mrs. Strong in sole charge of the shop. I arrived back to find her with that secret smile on her face which means she has sold something startling.

'Guess what?' she said.

'I'm too tired to play guessing games; put me out of my misery. Tell me what you've sold.'

'Look,' said Mrs. Strong, pointing to the top shelf where I had placed the Chinese figures.

The pornography in porcelain had gone.

'Heavens above, who on earth did you sell them to? Did they *know* . . .?' I asked.

'Oh yes, he knew all right,' replied Mrs. Strong. 'He knew what they were when he saw them through the window. He is a doctor and collects such things. If you have any more will you please ring him?'

Well, really! With schoolteachers collecting pornographic postcards and the medical profession buying doubtful porcelian figures, it makes one wonder, doesn't it?

I looked at the entry in the daybook and saw 'twenty-five pounds' entered against the sale of the figures.

'He paid *that* for *them*?' I said shakily.

'Certainly,' replied Mrs. Strong, with the cat-who-drank-the-cream look again on her face. 'Oh, he fought back a bit but it was take it or leave it as far as I was concerned.'

Well, I was thankful that he took them, but I can't help feeling that we had overdone the price a bit. Could they be worth twenty-five pounds to anyone? Apparently they could. Still, they were most beautiful bits of Chinese porcelain from the front view even if repellent from the base. I wondered which view he had considered was worth the price. It takes all sorts to make up this world of ours, and we seem to get a good share of odd folk in the shop. Mrs. Strong was quite elated about the sale. I asked if she intended to make a name for herself by specializing in pornographic porcelain. The remark took the cat-with-cream look from her face, all right.

Some days later I was alone in the shop when a most odd man walked in. He was very small and podgy, almost as broad as he was tall, with a cherubic face that so often goes with anyone so small in stature. I noticed that his tiny feet were encased in finely made, continental-type shoes. He was good-looking in a way and spoke with a thick accent. I summed him up as being probably of Italian parentage. His voice was falsetto in timbre which rather put me off.

'One of *those*,' I thought, but quite without any prejudice.

The customer enquired if I had any strange walking-sticks. Well, I always have a few odd items like this about the shop; walking-sticks that, when the knob is turned, a watch is shown or which pull out into a sword or yardstick. I showed him all that I had and it was one of the days when I could offer him a good selection. He looked at them, but without showing any real interest which might lead to a sale. We talked about this and that in a nonchalant manner; he knew a lot about antiques but in my mind I dismissed him as a time-waster. Yet he seemed to want to linger, even when I began to put away the walking-sticks. He sidled up to me, as graceful as a ballet dancer, his tight little shoes squeaking a bit as he moved.

He hesitated a moment and then said:

'Have you not any truly *odd* sticks?'

I began to sense something very odd about him but maybe I was wrong.

'If you will tell me exactly what you have in mind, perhaps I can be more helpful,' I replied primly but in my best efficient shop manner.

'What I really want . . .' Again the hesitation and then it came out in a burst of cross-bred English. 'What I really want is one of those sticks made of a bull's penis. . . .'

This was a time when I think I would have been justified in showing surprise but the training of years prevented this happening.

'You know the sort of thing?' he questioned. 'Sometimes they come from Africa, but I believe English farmers also made such things.'

He looked at me with watery pleading eyes. Well, I'd asked him bluntly enough to tell me what he wanted and he had certainly done so!

'Of course I know the sort of thing.' I was lying, but hoped it was not too blatant. 'Why, I had one a few weeks ago but it has gone now.'

'You *did*?' The falsetto voice was positively trilling. 'How wonderful! Oh, if you could find one for me I should be so happy. . . .'

I promised I would do so and he scribbled his address down. He became confidential and started off on a long hymn of praise on the beauties of walking-sticks made of bulls' penises. I was beginning to get a bit tired of the whole thing and wished he would go. After all, three adventures into the world of pornography within a month is quite enough for one shopkeeper. I produced my usual weapon of defence, the feather duster, and made a show of being busy. The little man was not to be put off by such a feeble gesture: he came within striking distance of the feather duster.

'I knew I could ask *you* about such a thing,' he said, all treacly and confidential. 'When I looked through the window I said to myself, "Now there is a woman who will understand me".'

Great heavens, I thought . . . here I am with my fortieth birthday a thing of the past, and a little Italian creature thinks I understand him!

The falsetto voice trilled on. 'I asked one woman once for a bull's penis. You know what? She looked at me as if I was dirt. But you, dear lady, you are *simpatica*, so *simpatica* I can talk to you.'

I felt anything but *simpatica*. Fortunately at this moment Mrs. Strong came back to the shop and the day was saved. The little man left, beaming and bowing. As he passed the window he stopped to wave a tiny, gaily gloved hand.

Mrs. Strong looked at me reprovingly.

'Boy friend of yours?' she asked laconically. 'What did he want?'

There are so few times when I can get the better of Mrs. Strong but this was going to be one of those times!

'Just a bull's penis,' I said airily.

Mrs. Strong looked just as I hoped she would—shattered.

'Gawd!' The cockney accent comes out when we are alone. ' 'Struth, what's he want that for?'

'For a walking-stick, of course,' I said, making it sound quite matter of fact.

This really got Mrs. Strong shaky; she could only make weak, murmuring noises.

'Didn't you know they make very good walking-sticks?'

She obviously did not believe me.

'Well,' she said resignedly, 'we've had the lot this month, haven't we? I reckon a bull's penis is just about the limit.'

I agreed with her. As I tore the last day of the month off the calendar, it was with relief.

Next month would be different; it was a sincere hope.

26
Carnival

IN RINGWOOD the high-light of our social calendar is the carnival. Do not be mistaken in thinking that this is a mere one-day affair. Following a year of preparation we have a full seven days of carnival revelry.

A right good time is had by everyone in the town, except possibly me. Our carnival takes place in September, generally about the second week of the month. In the whirl of being busy during the tourist months of July and August there has never been a year yet when the announcement of the carnival date did not come as a surprise to me. Suddenly I find myself on the fringe of being popular. People who haven't spoken to me for months suddenly peep round the shop door and say:

'Oh, have you any ostrich feathers? My daughter needs some for the carnival.'

I produce the ostrich feathers from the back room of the shop, generally entailing a great deal of thought in order to track them down and certainly with a fair amount of actual hard work in releasing them from some encumbrance.

Years ago I used to be quite naive and think that a head poked round the door asking for ostrich feathers meant a sale. Now I know differently. Although the residents of Ringwood take their carnival seriously, it seldom occurs to them actually to *buy* anything. For years I have had such hoary old remarks trotted out such as:

'Well, it's only for a day, can I borrow them?'

How mean can one get? I used to lend such things as ostrich feathers, feeling that one should contribute something to the carnival spirit.

For one carnival some years ago I lent numerous lamps and a considerable number of swords. In those days I was younger and less soured by business. I felt it was almost a privilege to lend anything that was required until I woke up to the fact that, after lending anything, it was always I who had to go to fetch the things back to the shop.

Once the carnival is over an awful sort of inertia sets in. The enthusiasm of borrowing does not stretch out to returning. This year my name went very low into the mud; I flatly refused to lend a single thing! People who are not in business themselves rarely realize that there are such people as myself who lead very busy lives. To lend one thing is nothing as it takes up very little of one's time. Multiply the article by fifty and it represents a considerable amount of man-power to collect goods up, pack them, etc. It is also quite unreasonable to expect anyone to lend even the most trivial of things if the lender has to spend time and money on 'phone calls making requests for the goods to be returned.

I have never had the time or inclination to join the many social groups in Ringwood who work all the year round for the various carnival committees. Frankly, committees scare me to death! I admire the people who are committee and community minded but I expect to reserve the right to decide that such a life is not for me. The result is that one can be regarded as an antisocial freak in a small market town such as ours. In point of fact, a business like this antique shop of mine is a demanding thing. The work really begins when the shop is closed. There is always stock to be sorted out and unexpected visits to be made into the country to look at stuff for sale. So, for the sake of building up a business from literally nothing, social occasions have to be limited.

Actually I love the carnival week as much as anyone. I pray as hard as anyone else for fine weather and someone's prayers must be very effective as we rarely have a wet carnival week.

To me the most exciting thing about the carnival is the advent of the fair into the town, for the fair brings one of the most remarkable women that I have ever had the privilege to meet.

She owns the fair, and Melita is a woman of magnetic quality. Melita comes to the shop as soon as she arrives in Ringwood and brings me news of many of the travelling people whom we both know. As I potter around the shop, dusting this article or replacing this, she talks and it is good to hear her voice. We may not meet for many months but we carry on the conversation as if it were a serial. Melita is a keen business woman herself. She has to be, for the modern fair is still a tough training ground for any woman to hold together. Melita is old, and has a store of stories about the old days of the fair which fascinate me. I can never have enough of her stories. The present fairs are pale, thin cousins of their robust ancestors, but they still have a cunning charm which is hard for a country person to withstand.

At night I have gone along to the fairground and I have seen Melita working as hard as any man. By contrast I have met her in a hotel magnificently dressed in green velvet with a fine mink stole slung casually round her lean shoulders. Her fingers have been covered with enormous rings that at first glance seem impossible to be real, but they are. Melita has never known any other life than that of the fairground and she loves to come to Ringwood.

''Tis a homely place,' she often says to me.

I rib her about the money she must be making and she retaliates by haggling with me over a piece of jewellery which she thinks she might buy—'if trade is good'. Trade always seems to be good, for she generally buys something and even our friendship survives the hard haggling between us.

'You're a hard woman to do a deal with,' I mutter, pretending to be sullen.

'Aye,' says Melita. 'But for a young 'un you ain't doing so bad yourself.'

Saturday is the real carnival day. There is a big parade through the streets with amazingly well decorated floats led by a silver band, the procession winds past the shop to the market-place and then to the field at the top of the town where the queen and her attendants watch the amusements in the arena. At night there is another procession, this time with many more floats and they are floodlit. Certainly it is the best carnival I have ever seen. Not quite in the Battle of Flowers class, but this is Ringwood, not Nice.

Of course, everyone is too intent on getting the last shred of enjoyment from our rural Mardi Gras to bother about buying anything. I have learnt from experience that it is better to be resigned to writing off carnival day as a dead loss as far as business is concerned.

The spirit of Carnival is with us. Think of the tourist season, the American invasion and the prospect of winter culminating in the rush of Christmas buyers. It is enough for any shop-keeper.

When the carnival procession has passed the door I generally fight my way through the madding crowds to the field. There is a distracting amount of noise and the smell of fish-and-chips vies with the hamburgers. These stalls fascinate me, the doubtful quality of meat is overpowered by the violence of the onions as the two meet on the battlefield of a stomach-filling hunk of bread. Eaten at the fairground the hamburger has been known to hold many aristocratic bodies and souls together sufficiently well to withstand the perilous whirligigs. On carnival day you can stand in the crowd, happily tearing away at a hamburger, to discover that your neighbour is a councillor whom you didn't vote for. Today you are united by a hamburger. For a moment you forget that this was the man who helped to vote against your application for a building permit. Even carnival day cannot prevent a last tiny dislike for the innocent representative of local bureaucracy. Better to move to the fairground itself.

Smells and noise and again the overpowering contact with sardine-packed humanity, as much a part of the fair as the raucous pleas of the sideshow owners to 'try their stalls'. The inhibitions of contemporary life can so easily be dispelled by anyone who dares to sample 'all the fun of the fair'.

I throw six hard balls at a row of perky, tow-headed coconuts and laugh out loud as I think how often I've wanted to do this during the last year. The hirsute coconut on the left looks exactly like someone I can't bear. I can't resist the temptation to buy another six balls. Whack! I aim accurately at the most hirsute coconut and score a bulls's-eye. The stallholder looks as surprised as I feel. The reward is more than a fine milky coconut to give to the children; I begin to feel relaxed. Later on in the evening the coconut becomes an embarrassment as I bump into people that I know.

As I am quite unable to drive a car, it is a wonderful feeling to know that I can climb into a bumper-car and race madly around. Forget the Highway Code; here it doesn't matter. The more you bump the better you feel. Look, there is the bobby who booked the van for parking the other week. Even a minor revenge is sweet in a bumper-car.

I toy with the idea of climbing to the top of the twisting tower then realize that this form of fairground pleasure is not for me. I have to content myself with watching the youth of the town struggling to hold down their skirts as they slide screamingly on a mat to the bottom. It's a popular place for the male youngsters to congregate indulging in a robust type of fun.

In the distance I can see Melita talking to a booth owner. She is paid 'pitch money' by the stall-owners for the privilege of setting up their stalls on the ground, but it is more than a business venture. It is a meeting of families from all the counties in the Southern Region.

The carnival ends in a flurry of fireworks cascading heavenwards in a myriad of many-coloured lights. As the last set-piece flares up in the centre of the field, the spirit of Carnival receives its *coup de grâce*.

It's all over bar the shouting. That goes on well into the night, but by church time on Sunday morning Ringwood is itself again.

During the next week Ringwood seems a dull market town again, but within a month the committees are meeting again. Another carnival is being planned and, all too soon, another year has passed. The groaning noise of the fairground people trundling their massive equipment through the narrow High Street is with us again. Another and yet another carnival week comes to Ringwood and with it the revelry of our rural Mardi Gras. The collecting-boxes rattle as the clowns invade each shop in the High Street.

It is the same every year. The strange thing is that I never feel a year older in carnival week!

27
Madame, please don't put your daughter into antiques

'MUMMY,' said the teenager with the Marylin Monroe qualifications of vital statistics, 'Mummy, isn't this *the* most adorable shop?'

'Mummy' turned to me and said:

'Vera has always loved antique shops, even when she was quite a tiny girl. I promised to let her have one when she was old enough.'

This simple conversation took my breath away. How wonderful it must be to have a parent who could blithely promise to give its offspring an antique shop, but it certainly set me thinking. How, for instance, did one arrive at the right age to acquire an antique shop? Is it enough to find this type of shop 'adorable'? I think this is far from being true.

During the course of the year I hear many people rave over the advantages of owning a shop such as mine. It has never struck me as being a particularly glamorous profession, perhaps because I know too much about the seedy side of it. There are many days when I am quite certain there are much easier ways of earning a living. It is pleasant to be able to buy nice things even if they ultimately have to be sold, and that, I think, is the crux of the matter. Every would-be aspirant to own an antique shop that I have met recently always says, quite naively:

'Oh, I'd never part with some of these beautiful things, I couldn't bear it.'

I regret that for this person there is a whale of a lot of heartache in store if they ever have a shop such as mine. First and foremost, the temptation to buy only the things that you like personally has to be eliminated. It may not happen the first year, but it is inevitable. Personally I cannot stand Staffordshire figures of any kind, for my own pleasure I would never buy one at all. As a shopkeeper I know that the buying public shows a great interest in such things. If I have Staffordshire figures in the shop I sell them. So, in this way, the first crude taste of commercialism rears its ugly head. It would be delightful to say that I kept a shop purely for aesthetic pleasure; it *ought* to be like that but it is far from true. The acme of perfection is really to be born a millionairess with sufficient taste to buy lovely, fine-quality antiques. To be born a shopkeeper with only the ability to find them and sell them can leave the tiniest trace of bitterness in one's mouth. Beauty and art go hand in hand, commercialism makes a bad third party.

Not only the young sometimes feel the urge to own an antique shop; no age is really immune from being bitten by the bug. There are regiments of middle-aged women who think the idea is rather 'fun'. It is one thing to sell a piece of Victorian jewellery or a bit of silver bought at a sale to a friend, or even a friend of a friend. There are many middle-aged ladies living in private houses in this area who have lots of fun in this way. They attend sales, pretending to buy the odd bit of furniture for their house which is already over-furnished. They dabble, like amateur painters, in a dangerous subject which ultimately gets too big for them. Once a shop is acquired, buying and selling takes on a very different aura to the little tea-party sales amongst friends. The overheads of a shop are considerable. Once a shop door is open, an antique dealer is bound to stock a very wide variety of objects.

She may have five thousand things in the shop for sale, and one day every customer who comes into the shop can ask for six or seven different objects that she is lacking. Frustration can set in unless the distinction is clearly defined between the serious antique *shopkeeper* and the dilettante Madame X who is rather clever at buying a few things at sales to sell to friends.

Also, in a shop, there comes the terrible time when your own personal friends bring goods in for you to buy. It can be a most embarrassing experience. I have had people whom I know personally bringing some small object to the shop which I know they value highly. Alas, when viewed in the cold light of commercial trading it has little or no value. There arises the problem of letting a friend down as lightly as possible, or of acquiring her little 'treasure' at the expense of her friendship. I know too well how quickly one can build up a reputation for being 'as hard as nails', it is possibly the easiest thing in the world. Gradually I find myself withdrawing more and more from any ties of friendship, as the shop becomes more and more demanding on both my time, money and personality.

So when I hear a young girl expressing a wish to have an 'adorable shop' like this one the seeds of worry are set in me. Are they prepared to take the frightening disillusionment which can come even in the best of shops? I look at the silver copper and brass, shining brightly as it stands in the window, and I wonder how the sweet girls would tackle the problem of facing a mountain of dirty silver at perhaps seven o'clock at night after a hectic day's work? For, although buffing machines can be used on a lot of metal objects, it is the final touch of good old elbow-grease that really brings it to the perfection which customers like to see when it is finally displayed in the cabinets of the shop. Buying and selling antiques has never been, and never will be, a nine-till-five steady occupation. There is always furniture to be moved, to be cleaned until the old patina shows through; always a mass of china in the back room to be sorted out, washed, checked and priced; always metals to be polished.

I do all my buying myself, and this frequently entails long and tiring journeys. Hours have to be spent poring over catalogues from salerooms many miles apart, and sales require planning almost with military precision. Some salerooms will attract the 'vultures' from everywhere and you can be certain that prices will be sky-high, especially when you get the local ring battling against the London ring. The lone wolf from a little shop has to plan to go to a sale where there is a reasonable chance to earn a day's wage and which will cover travelling expenses as well. It is nerve-racking to spend a day in some dismal saleroom, going practically on to your knees to try to buy the right kind of goods at the right price to enable one to make a profit. Every antique dealer aims to buy his goods at a price that he can sell again into the 'trade' if not to the public. Goods in the 'trade' don't make a very high price, for generally everyone knows how much has originally been paid for the article.

When I first started this shop I used to run it single-handed. Now, after various trials at finding a suitable assistant, I have got Mrs. Strong. She has a rare sensibility to make the right decisions during my absence, and so I am fortunate in being able to spend days away from the shop knowing that it will be efficiently run. I had several assistants before Mrs. Strong; some of them left me to start up on their own in 'antiques or second-hand goods', but within three months I have had a frantic call from them to buy them out lock, stock and barrel. They saw only the glamour of the shop, and forgot the drudgery and the responsibility. I suppose, on the surface, any antique shop looks all honey and cream, it seems such an easy way to make a living.

A customer comes to the shop and it is a great feeling to sell something, whether the price is high or not. It looks so simple, to sit in a nice shop until a customer comes along to buy something. Actually, it is the end-product of years of care, thought and even studying, the culminating point of hours of hard graft, the reward for hard work!

Some of the young girls who express a liking to work in an antique shop would be a physical wreck after one normal week here. After a busy day I find myself looking round the shop with something like dismay. Is it only a few hours ago when this shop looked so neat and tidy? At five o'clock a hundred articles are disarranged, there are fingermarks on the silver, gaps on the walls where pictures and plates have been sold. Many long treks have to be made up and down stairs to find more stock to replace the stuff that has been sold. Furniture may perhaps have to be taken from the shop to be delivered into the country. It is so easy to sell an expensive cabinet, ignoring the fact that it is full of china at the time. The painful part begins when the china has to be taken out and the cabinet carefully extricated from the bulging shop. Then there is the little matter of finding another cabinet to rehouse the china. Ten minutes were needed to persuade the client that this cabinet was just what she needed, but perhaps four hours are needed to fill the gap. The only truly cheerful thing to do at this point, when spirits are at their lowest ebb, is to count the takings in the till and hope that they are sufficient to warrant such an upheaval.

Not very long ago I had a customer who deserves a medal in a marathon event. Carelessly leaving the door open one Thursday afternoon, I went upstairs to hear the shop bell ring within a minute of my settling down for a 'quiet half day', Thursday being our normal early closing day. I went downstairs to find an elderly lady in the shop, already beginning to enjoy herself by poking around the bric-à-brac. The time was 2.30. The lady went through everything that she could see in the shop, we fortified ourselves with numerous cups of tea. At 9 p.m. she was still poking around, this time amongst the prints. It was gratifying to be handed a very substantial cheque at 10 p.m. Then we set about packing up her purchases. She decided to take all the small stuff with her. We spent three hours packing it! The furniture we sent on about a week later. It took just about a week to set out the shop again. There was also about four hours' work putting back the stuff which she had dug out and then changed her mind about! Perhaps we both should have a medal for that afternoon's work. I know I ended up with my feet in a bowl of bath salts; it took me days to get them back into shape again!

So, unless your daughter is absolutely physically fit, don't give her an antique shop to play about in, please, madame. Buy her loads of glossy magazines on antiques, let her have a little flutter in the salerooms by all means. Let her enjoy the treasures in your home or even sell a few things to your neighbours, but be wary of actually working in a shop such as mine. It puts years on your life, adds wrinkles to the forehead which only a permanent Helena Rubinstein on the staff can eliminate successfully, and she is sure to have varicose veins before she is thirty.

Madame, if your daughter is fearfully precocious and declares that she will die, but most certainly die, unless she is allowed to work in an antique shop, then be firm with her. Use your influence and try to get her a job in a museum. In such a place she will get a thoroughly good grounding and, if she can stay the pace, in a few years' time she will be tough enough to be let loose in a shop.

Indulge her whim to this extent and you may find yourself with a daughter who can support you in your old age, and you will certainly save a lot of money. If she can survive working in a museum you will find you have gained a pearl beyond price, and have something well worth offering to any antique dealer or art gallery in any part of the world. She will be armed with knowledge and be quite capable of holding her own in the jungle such as antiques become when they are commercialized. If she falters on the way she will still be young enough to take up another job. The knowledge which she will be bound to pick up will never be lost.

I do not think that anyone can ever learn antiques by merely working in a shop. A child who is born 'in the trade' often turns out to have a flair for the business. At an early age a child may hear its parents discussing business deals and there is a reasonable chance that they will take a great interest in a family shop. The chances are equal though that, even if you have a chain of art galleries or shops, a son or daugher may set his or her heart on being an atomic scientist. It is a two-way gamble, but I really feel that the odds are slightly in favour of the children who are bred and brought up in the trade. They lose a lot of their childhood at perhaps too early an age, but it is an occupational risk.

Madame, I plead with you, don't put your daughter into antiques in sheer cold blood. Think hard before you take the step of buying her shop for herself. Change your mind in that delightfully tantalizing manner which you have when you are a customer in an antique shop. It is a vocation, not only in occupation, dear lady. Believe me, it is much more fun to be footloose and fancy-free as a customer in someone else's shop.

An antique shop is a tiny bit of heaven surrounded by an awfully large piece of hell.

28
Another shop
in another High Street

ALL the great events of my life seem to take place in September. Both my sons were born in this month and it has always been a month of contrasts. So when September 1960 came along I was surprised to find myself in a slightly debilitated state of mind. We had had a heavy season and now all the excitement of the shop was ebbing away. There was, as it were, a great lull in my life, and a lull such as this is always a portent to something impressive, a curtain-raiser to an epic!

On the pavement outside our shop one Wednesday I met one of my landlords. Our conversation lasted perhaps five minutes.

'You ought to see our new shop in Chard. It would be just the place for you,' he said.

I was jaundiced with everything. Politely I murmured something about 'one day I'll go to Chard' (and in truth I once tried to go there but the car broke down miles from nowhere and I had to walk, a million miles—*back*).

I can't drive a car myself and this is often a great *advantage* in not going to a place. It has been many a time my escape route when I was not very interested in a thing. On this occasion it was not to be.

'Aha,' says my landlord. 'I'll drive you there myself.'

This in itself rather took the wind from my sails, and before one could say 'a year's rent in advance' we had fixed a date to go to Chard.

We arranged to go on the following Monday. Vaguely, I

spent the next few days dreaming up excuses for *not* going, for I was pining to be in Nice. The weather was atrocious and I had a big hate on me. In short I was in a bad-tempered sulk (can't for the life of me think what about!).

When I had toyed with every possible excuse for not going I thought blithely, 'Oh, well, my dear landlord will probably forget anyway,' and left the matter to fate. But my landlord did not forget. Even more miraculously, he arrived exactly on time, and the only virtue I appreciate is a fanatical regard for promptness. Ten o'clock to me is ten o'clock, not one minute before or after. This completely unnerved me, and away we went to Chard.

It was a ghastly day; the country was shrouded in mist and any chance of enjoying the scenery was doomed. I saw sixty miles of gloom ahead of me, and sixty miles back. We'll hate each other like mad after this, I thought. After all, the only landlord I ever really knew well was a Bavarian gamekeeper in Switzerland, and we had terrible Germanic conversations together and frightful arguments as he insisted that there were *no* concentration camps in Germany during the war. So I was rather prejudiced against the possible social attributes of any landlord.

The conversation with my present landlord had none of these controversial angles. We started with the weather (my landlord is very English) and passed on to yachts, holidays abroad, the vagaries of the French as a nation; aspects of religion embracing Protestantism, Roman Catholicism, Jews and sundry Oriental types; the education system, virtues of putting children into universities; the Stock Exchange; the advantages and disadvantages of having money; problems of junior delinquents, and ultimately back to the weather again. This latter subject was rather forced upon us for we literally fell into Chard in a cloudburst plus a thunderstorm. It was something of a minor triumph to have made the trip at all!

I stumbled, stiff from sitting in the car, out into the road and saw—*it*. Another shop in another High Street; another wavy roof and around it again the sombre air of neglect and lack of affection. A sad, weeping little shop obviously longing for a tenant. Through the lush luxury of a carpeted shop (the part occupied by my landlord) we entered into the cold damp corridor of the shop. Again the flapping wallpaper, the crinkle of wood-wormed floors.

A staircase of rather surprising width and elegance drifted tiredly into the shop itself surmounted by a fanlight window. Amazingly, the thunder and lightning had stopped and a shud-dering beam of sunlight came through the fanlight. And at that moment I saw it as it could be. A gleaming white staircase which would triumphantly become part of the shop; a background to gleaming silver and crystal chandeliers, the subtle reflection of light against the contrasting patina of gleaming furniture. Certainly it must have this fusion of light against light. Give this place more light in every way than it had seen for many a year and it would take on a new aura of happiness, and therefore would be a success. I smiled at my landlord, but he did not see the things that I saw and was already becoming restless and time-conscious.

So we started again on the homeward journey and interspersed the conversation with details about length of a lease, the rent, the commitments of landlord and tenant. To me the only important thing was to convert the ugly duckling in the High Street of Chard into a veritable glamorous swan, and quickly—quickly. Forget the lease, the letters to lawyers, throw prudence (that destroyer of freedom) to the winds, forget the plasterless walls, the long wet journey! Time would bring every imaginable problem along in due course. There would be battles; visits to surveyors and council offices, but it would end the way I wanted it. White and strong and shining, like a dream. That's it, a dream. Build madly, another trailing cloud of glory weaving a silver thread into the drabness of Big Business. Ultimately it all has to be translated into terms of money, but today see only the dream-like quality. Tomorrow and the next day you will swear in six different languages and make screaming noises on the telephone to solicitors and argue about the rent. You will tear great hand-fuls of hair from your head because the builder does not work quickly enough. You will reach the period when none of it will be worth while, *but* you will go on, driven by the old tearing urgency in you to create something from nothing. A need to breathe life into the cold walls of a decaying shop. An escape route from boredom, another shop in another High Street.

* * * * *

It drops through the letter-box with a more pretentious sound than a bill or an income-tax demand note.

This is how it all began, surely? Somewhere I have seen these words before. . .?

My husband slipped a parcel into my hand. It was the latest Sabicas record!

Tell me, dear reader, have *you* read any good leases lately? Play the Flamenco music of Sabicas; hand me the Sauterne and drink lustily to the success of another shop in another High Street, to Chard, in Somerset, in England.

Iraqis regarded returning exiles with suspicion, convinced that they automatically wanted to be become leaders in Iraq after living in luxury hotels in exile, supported by foreign intelligence services. Abdul Mohsin al-Kafaji – a former colonel in the Iraqi army who joined the Shia uprising and later became a close aide to al-Khoie – admitted that at first people were nervous at seeing them, particularly as Baghdad had not yet fallen. 'They were frightened that Saddam might come back and said, "Maybe the same thing will happen as in 1991." But day by day the number of people coming to the shrine with us increased.' Al-Khoie told people not to resist the Americans and distributed $350,000 to the poor of Najaf.

On the morning of April 10, al-Khoie took a dangerous step as part of his campaign to reconcile different factions in Najaf. He went to the house of Haidar al-Rufaie al-Killidar and asked him to come with him to the shrine. Haidar was not popular in Najaf, where his family had for centuries been the hereditary custodians of the shrine of Imam Ali, the son-in-law of the Prophet Muhammad, murdered in 661 and venerated by Shias. To be custodian of the shrine was not an easy job. Radwan Hussein al-Rufaie, a cousin of Haidar, said: 'I turned it down because I was against the regime and my brother took over, but he disappeared in 1991, accused of plotting against the regime. Haidar on the other hand was seen as completely affiliated with the government. He appeared on television talking with Saddam Hussein and was a member of the Iraqi parliament.' Haidar had very sensibly not been to his office since the war began. But, looking nervous, he agreed to return there.

Al-Khoie and the group of clerics and supporters with him arrived at the shrine at about 8.45 a.m. A friendly crowd greeted them as they passed through the great gates of the shrine complex, walked across a stone-paved courtyard and prayed by the shrine itself. They then went to sit in al-Killidar's smart-looking office. The last photograph of al-Khoie still alive shows him sitting there. He is smiling gently but confidently at his companions.

Outside in the courtyard of the shrine an hour passed before there were the first signs of hostility. A crowd gathered and there were shouts of 'Long life to al-Sadr' and 'Give us Haidar or we will kill you.' At first al-Khoie tried to calm the crowd, which by now numbered about 400, but the microphone he was trying to use did not work. One man lunged at him with a knife as he stood at the door of the custodian's office and he jumped back. Al-Kafaji says the first shot was fired into the air by Maher al-Naseri, a cleric from Detroit, where there is a large Iraqi community, and a companion of al-Khoie who had travelled with him to Iraq. 'He became frightened and fired a shot. Many in the crowd ran away, but only to get their own guns.' There were two Kalashnikovs and two pistols in Haidar's office. Both sides began to shoot. In the exchange of fire al-Naseri was mortally wounded. Al-Khoie took off his turban and held it to his chest, shouting: 'Don't shoot! This young man is dying! He is a Shia! He is a Muslim!'

The shooting went on for ninety minutes. Ma'ad Fayan, who fired a pistol at somebody trying to get through the door, recalls: 'Somebody threw a grenade. I heard Sayid Majid [al-Khoie] call out: "I am hurt."' One of his fingers had been blown off and another was dangling by a piece of skin. Fayad tried to staunch the bleeding with a towel. The siege ended when al-Khoie's group ran out of ammunition and one man went outside with a white shirt and a Koran to surrender. Some of the crowd entered the office and tied the hands of those inside behind their backs. Shaikh Salah Bilal, one of those captured, says he was told by one of the men: 'We are taking you to Muqtada al-Sadr for him to pass sentence.' The prisoners were then taken out of the office. Ma'ad Fayan recalls: 'The first thing I saw was swords and knives flashing in the sun. I thought, "Oh my God, that's it."' Within minutes he saw Haidar al-Rufaie stabbed to death and al-Khoie repeatedly stabbed. Muqtada's house was a few hundred yards away from the shrine. Al-Khoie slumped by his door. 'Most of his body was bleeding and he lay down on one side,' says Shaikh

Salah. 'I put his head on my leg.' After some minutes, he says, a message came from al-Sadr: 'Don't let them sit in front of my door.' They took refuge in a shop which sold sewing machines where their hands were untied. The owner of the shop tried to save them by telling the crowd outside that al-Khoie was dead. It did not work; after some minutes he was dragged out of the shop and shot dead at the end of the street. According to one source al-Khoie's body was dragged behind a car before it was returned to his relatives for burial. The savagery of his own death matched al-Khoie's worst expectations about divisions between Iraqis. Saddam Hussein might fall, but the killings in the shadow of the Imam Ali shrine showed that hatreds between Iraqis were so deep that the bloodshed might only be beginning.

VIII

A SMEAR OF DARK blood on the dusty pavement marked the spot where an American soldier had been killed by a bullet in the neck and another wounded in the arm. Gunmen had shot the soldiers as they stood guard at Mahdia gas station not far from the al-Dohra power station with its four tall chimneys in south Baghdad. A crowd of a dozen Iraqi men, some of whom had seen the shooting, were peering at the rusty-brown blood-stains, already baked hard by the heat of the midsummer sun, and talking about what had happened. Without exception they all said they approved of the attack. 'We think they deserved it,' said a man called Muhammad Abbas with quiet earnestness. 'We admire the bravery of those who attacked them.' Another bystander, who refused to give his name, pointed to the American helicopters swooping and diving above our heads, commenting: 'Nobody cares when an Iraqi civilian is killed but as soon as an American dies there are lots of American helicopters flying about.' A third man added, to nods of approval from the rest of the crowd, that his family was very poor but 'We will celebrate by cooking a chicken. God willing there will be more actions like this.' Al-Dohra is a large, mostly Sunni Arab district in south Baghdad which was to become a centre for the insurgents over the next three years. It is easily accessible across thickly populated agricultural land to militant nationalist and Islamic fundamentalist or Salafi villages further to the south. By